I0119897

Anonymous

The Art of Modern Lace-Making

Anonymous

The Art of Modern Lace-Making

ISBN/EAN: 9783743401921

Manufactured in Europe, USA, Canada, Australia, Japa

Cover: Foto ©Andreas Hilbeck / pixelio.de

Manufactured and distributed by brebook publishing software
(www.brebook.com)

Anonymous

The Art of Modern Lace-Making

THE ART

OF

MODERN LACE-MAKING.

PRICE:

FIFTY CENTS OR TWO SHILLINGS.

PUBLISHED BY

THE BUTTERICK PUBLISHING CO. (LIMITED).

LONDON AND NEW YORK.

PRINTED IN NEW YORK.

INTRODUCTION.

~~~~~~~~~~

Owing to the growing popularity of the fascinating art of lace-making and the appeals of our readers to place it within their reach, we have prepared this pamphlet. In making it a perfect instructor and a reliable exponent of the favorite varieties of lace, we have spared neither time nor expense, and are most happy to offer to our patrons what a celebrated maker of Modern Lace has pronounced as "the finest book upon lace-making to be found on either continent."

The illustrations, in the main, are direct reproductions from genuine, hand-made modern laces, such as any lady may make who masters the instructions found upon these pages.

The beauty of these laces is beyond question, their durability all that can be desired, and their textures may be varied from an extreme delicacy to a sumptuous opposite. In introducing the art of modern lace-making into the realms of our readers. we feel all of the pleasure we are sure we thus convey.

THE BUTTERICK PUBLISHING CO.,
Limited.

CONTENTS.

Lace-Making

ANCIENT AND MODERN METHODS.

THE art of making lace in one form or another has existed from the earliest ages. There are Scriptural references to various web-like fabrics, which were of rude construction, no doubt, but whose general characteristics were identical with those productions of modern skill which have for centuries been known as lace. Homer and other ancient writers constantly mention net-works of fancifully embroidered materials; gold thread-work was known to the Romans; and as Egyptian robes of state are depicted upon the tombs of the earlier dynasties as being fashioned from a looped net-work or crochet, it is probable that the Israelites learned the art from the Egyptians. Museums contain specimens of lace dating back to periods that to us of the present day seem mere dreams of reigns and eras, and history includes a scattered literature of lace which proves that the art must have been practised almost from the beginning.

Up to the Sixteenth Century, however, open work embroidery was the favorite decoration, and from it the tangible origin of lace seems derived. During the Renaissance period the first book of embroidery patterns and lace-work appeared. The earliest volume bearing a date was printed at Cologne in 1527; and it was during the reign of Richard III. of England that the word lace was first used in the descriptions of the royal wardrobe.

At first the best known laces were those of Venice, Milan and Genoa. The Italians claim the invention of point or needle-made lace; but the Venetian point is now a product of the past, and England and France supply most of the fine laces of the present time.

Lace-makers in the various European countries are trained to the work from child-hood; but it is said that the makers of Honiton lace, the fabric of which Queen Victoria's wedding gown was made, are rapidly decreasing in numbers, so that there are few persons now living who understand the construction of this exquisite "pillow" lace. The costly point and Honiton and the dainty Mechlin and Valenciennes of bygone days can only be produced by trained lace-workers, whose skilful fingers weave bobbins of cobweb-like thread to and fro over the "pillow" necessary to antique methods; and for this reason fine lace-making is practically beyond the skill of the amateur. Besides, some of the threads in the very filmy laces are so fine that they cannot be successfully manipulated except in a moist atmosphere, such as that of Great Britain; and even there some of the more exquisite specimens must perforce be made in underground rooms, since it is only there that the proper degree of moisture can be obtained. In dry climates these gossamer-like threads would roughen and break at almost the slightest touch.

Referring to the known origin of some of the earlier laces, a writer upon the subject says:

"They say it was a woman, Barbara Uttmann, who invented pillow lace in the 16th century. Women have ever been patrons of lace-making. Victoria has kept the Honiton laces in fashion, and it was the Duchess of Argyle who introduced lace-making in Scotland. The Countess of Erne and Lady Denny and Lady Bingham began it in Ireland, and Lady De Vere gave her own Brussels point for patterns when the first Irish point was made at Curragh. It was Elizabeth of Denmark who introduced lace-making in that country, and the Archduchess Sophia who started lace schools in Bohemia. "Now at least I can have laces," said Anne of Austria, when Louis XIII., her husband died, and her court was famous for its cleanliness and its Spanish point. Colbert had three women as coadjutors when he started lace-making in France. It was because Josephine loved point d'Alençon that Napoleon revived it. Eugenie spent $5,000 for a single dress flounce, and had $1,000,000 in fine laces."

Victoria's favorite, Honiton, is not considered a particularly beautiful lace, although its weaving is so tedious and difficult. "Real Honiton laces," so says an authority, "are made up of bits and bits fashioned by many different women in their own little cottages—here a leaf, there a flower, slowly woven through the long, weary days, only to be united afterward in the precious web by other workers who never saw its beginning. There is a pretty lesson in the thought that to the perfection of each of these little pieces the beauty of the whole is due—that the rose or leaf some humble peasant woman wrought carefully, helps to make the fabric worthy the adorning of a queen or the decoration of an altar, even as the sweetness and patient perfection in any life makes all living more worthy and noble. A single flower upon which taste and fancy were lavished, and which sustained and deft labor brought to perfection, represents the lives of many diligent women workers.

It has become so much the fashion to worship all things ancient that most lovers of fine lace would prefer to have it a century old; and yet there never was a time when laces were more beautiful, more artistic and more unique in design than just at the present day; for modern laces preserve the best features of the laces that have gone before them, and have added so many new inspirations that except for the sentiment, the romance or the history connecting this scrap with a title, that with a famous beauty, and another with some cathedral's sacred treasure, the palm would certainly be given to the gauze-like production of the poor flax thread spinner of the present day."

Not all people know the difference between point lace which is made with the needle, and pillow lace which is made with the bobbins—but much of the beautiful point lace of the present day is made with the needle, and its beauty stands a favorable comparison with the more costly pillow lace.

Strictly modern lace-making is a result of American ingenuity, and it has so simple a basis and is so easy to learn that any woman of average skill may, with little difficulty, produce by its different processes, laces that are really magnificent and quite as substantial and useful as they are exquisitely beautiful. In America modern lace-making has been developed to a high degree of perfection by its pioneer, Mrs. Grace B. McCormick, in whose designing rooms at No. 923 Broadway, New York, may be seen specimens of modern laces of every variety, from dainty needle-point to a very elaborate kind known as the Royal Battenburg. This English name for an American production was selected in honor of the Battenburg nuptials, which occurred about the time a patent for making the lace was applied for at Washington. Only a few years have elapsed since this plucky little woman made a single piece of lace edging from common braid as an experiment, and sold it for a trifling sum. Love for the work and perseverance have enabled her to overcome obstacles that would have discouraged a woman of ordinary energy, and she has gradually improved upon her earlier methods until modern lace occupies a front rank among the numerous dainty forms of needle-work of the day.

One of the finest specimens lately placed on exhibition is a table-cloth intended for use at elaborate dinners. It is made of the finest table linen and Royal Battenburg lace. The cloth is, of course, very large, and the lace, in the form of wide insertion, is let in above the border and is also arranged to divide the center into three squares. An outside border of edging to match completes this exquisite production, which has been two years in course of construction, and is valued at four hundred and seventy-five dollars. The same style of lace may be made by any one who studies the art and in any width or form, and it may be produced in many textures, although really intended for heavy effects. The making of such lace possesses a great charm for womankind in general, and will undoubtedly retain favor as long as needlecraft remains a pastime and employment with the gentler sex.

MATERIALS.

The requirements of modern lace-making are few. The products are classed as Honiton, Point, Duchesse, Princesse, Royal Battenburg or Old English Point, etc., etc.; but all are made with various braids arranged in different patterns and connected by numerous kinds of stitches, many different stitches often appearing in one variety of lace.

The materials required are neither numerous nor expensive. The following is a complete list: Tracing cloth, leather or *toile cirée*, lace braids of various kinds, linen thread, two or three sizes of needles, a good thimble and a pair of fine sharp scissors.

For each kind of lace there is a special sort of braid in various patterns, and the selection of the thread depends entirely upon the variety and quality of lace to be made. This selection should be left to the decision of the teacher or the skilled maker of laces, as she knows from experience the proper combinations of materials. Thus, in making Honiton and point lace, thread in twelve different degrees of fineness is used; and as the braids also vary in size, the thread must always be adapted to the braid. For Battenburg lace the thread is in eight sizes, the finest being used only for "whipping curves" or drawing edges into the outlines required. The "Ideal Honiton" is a new lace made with fancy Honiton braid and wash-silk floss in dainty colors, and is exquisite for doilies, mats, table scarfs and center-pieces.

Designs sold by lace-makers are usually drawn upon tracing cloth, as this is flexible and much more agreeable to work upon than any other material. The tracing cloth, when the braid is arranged, is basted to a foundation of leather or *toile cirée;* or smooth wrapping-paper may be basted under the design and will furnish all the support that is necessary, while being lighter than the *toile cirée.*

It must be remembered that the work is really wrong side out while in progress, so that it will not show its true beauty until finished and removed from the foundation or pattern. According to the braid and thread selected, these laces may be made of fairy-like fineness or of massive elegance—general results being dainty enough for the gown of a bride or sumptuous enough for the adornment of an altar.

Lace-making establishments will furnish designs of any width or shape desired, and will also originate designs for special articles for which there are only occasional calls. Regular edging designs are ordinarily made in four widths—from quite narrow to very wide; and not infrequently a handkerchief design is enlarged sufficiently to form a square for a table or a fancy stand.

In filling in the spaces of any design or pattern, the worker may choose the stitches that please her best, if she does not like those accompanying the design that she has selected or that has been sent her.

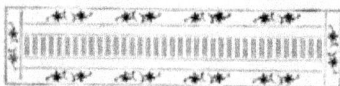

STITCHES USED IN MODERN LACE-MAKINE.

As in all fancy work which has a set of foundation stitches peculiar to it that may be varied according to the proficiency and ingenuity of the maker, so has Modern Lace a series of primary stitches from which may be evolved many others. A large number of illustrations of stitches, some of which are primary or foundation stitches, while others are combinations, are here presented, with full instructions for making; and the entire series given will make perfectly plain to the student the ease with which she may combine or invent stitches, when those of the design she is to work are not to her liking. The first stitch given is the main foundation stitch.

No. 1.—POINT DE BRUXELLES (BRUSSELS POINT).

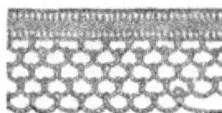

No. 2.—POINT DE BRUXELLES WORKED IN ROWS.

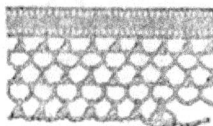

No. 3.—POINT DE VENISE (VENICE POINT).

No. 4.—PETIT POINT DE VENISE (LITTLE VENICE POINT).

PLAIN POINT STITCHES.

NOS. 1 AND 2.—POINT DE BRUXELLES OR BRUSSELS POINT.—Among the stitches most used in lace-making is Point de Bruxelles or Brussels point. It is simply a button-hole stitch worked loosely, and it must be done with regularity, as the beauty of the work depends almost wholly upon the evenness of the stitches. Brussels point is occasionally used as an edge, but is more frequently seen in rows worked back and forth to fill in spaces, or as a ground work. The illustrations clearly represent the method of making this stitch.

NO. 3.—POINT DE VENISE, OR VENICE POINT.—This stitch is worked from left to right, like Brussels point. Work 1 loose button-hole stitch, and in this stitch work 4 button-hole stitches tightly drawn up, then work another loose button-hole stitch, then 4 more tight button-hole stitches in the loose one; repeat to the end of the row, and fasten off.

NO. 4.—PETIT POINT DE VENISE, OR LITTLE VENICE POINT.—This stitch is worked in the same manner as point de Venise, but one tight stitch only is worked in each loose button-hole stitch. This is a most useful stitch for filling in small spaces.

NO. 5.—ITALIAN LACE STITCH.—Commence at the right side and pass the thread to the left.

First row.—Make a loose button-hole stitch into the braid to form a loop, then pass the needle under the line of thread, making the loops an eighth of an inch apart.

Second row.—Pass the thread back to the left, make a button-hole stitch in every loop, and pass the needle under the line of thread after each button-hole stitch.

No. 5.—ITALIAN LACE STITCH.

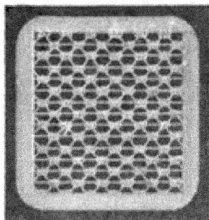

No. 6.—COBWEB LACE STITCH.

(For Directions see next Page.)

No. 6.—COBWEB LACE STITCH.—Commence at the right side, pass the thread to the left, work 3 button-hole stitches, miss the space of 3, which will leave a small loop, and continue these details to the end.

Second row.—Pass the thread back to the left side, work 3 button-hole stitches in each loop, taking up the line of thread with the loop, as seen in the engraving.

No. 7.—POINT BRABANÇON.—This stitch is worked as follows from left to right :

First row.—Make 1 long, loose point de Bruxelles, and 1 short loose one alternately, to end of row.

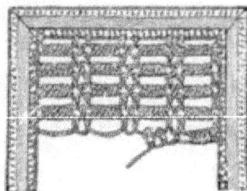

NO. 7.—POINT BRABANÇON.

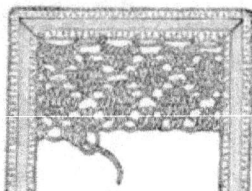

NO. 8.—POINT DE VALENCIENNES
(VALENCIENNES STITCH).

Second row.—Make 7 tight point de Bruxelles in the 1 long, loose stitch, and 2 short, loose point de Bruxelles in the short. loose stitch on previous row, and repeat across the row.

Third row.—Same as first.

No. 8.—POINT DE VALENCIENNES, OR VALENCIENNES STITCH.—This stitch appears complicated, but is really easy to work. Begin at the left hand and work 6 point de Bruxelles stitches at unequal distances, every alternate stitch being the larger.

Second row.—Upon the first large or long stitch, work 9 close button-hole stitches, then 1 short point de Bruxelles stitch under the one above, then 9 close stitches, and so on to the end of the row (right to left).

Third row.—Make 5 close button-hole stitches in the 9 of previous row, 1 short point de Bruxelles, 2 close, in the Bruxelles stitch, 1 short point de Bruxelles, 5 close, 1 short point de Bruxelles, 2 close, 1 short, 5 close, 1 short and repeat.

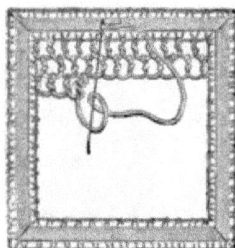

NO. 9.—POINT D' ESPAGNE
(SPANISH POINT).

Fourth row.—Make 5 close, 1 short point de Bruxelles, 2 close, 1 short, 5 close, 1 short, 2 close, 1 short, and repeat. Continue the rows until sufficient of the pattern is worked.

No. 9.—POINT D'ESPAGNE, OR SPANISH POINT.—This variety of stitch is worked from left to right as follows : Insert the needle in the edge of the braid, keeping the thread turned to the right, and bringing it out inside

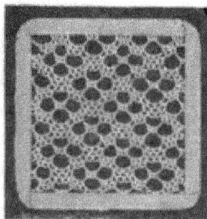

NO. 10.—GENOA LACE STITCH.

NO. 11.—FLEMISH LACE STITCH.
(For Directions see next Page.)

the loop formed by the thread (see illustration No. 9); the needle must pass from the back of the loop through it. Pass the needle under the stitch and bring it out in front, thus twice twisting the thread, which produces the cord-like appearance of this stitch. At the end of each row fasten to the braid and sew back, inserting the needle once in every open stitch.

No. 10.—GENOA LACE STITCH.—Commence at the right side, and work as follows :

First row.—Work 4 button-hole stitches, miss the space of 3, work 3, miss the space of 3, work 4. Continue to the end.

Second row.—Work 9 stitches close together, 3 into the spaces of the 4, and 3 more into the loop at each side of it. Miss the 3 stitches, and make 9 as before.

Third row.—Make 9 close stitches, 3 into the last 3 spaces of the 9, 3 into the loop, and 3 into the first spaces of the 9 next, and so on to the end.

Fourth row.—Repeat the first, loop, and the 4 into the center

No. 11.—FLEMISH LACE right side, and work as follows: hole stitches close together, miss space of 8; this will leave a large

Second row.—Make 8 button- and 2 in the small ones.

row, making 2 stitches in each

No. 12.—POINT DE FILLET, —This stitch is also represented method of making the knot is ground-work where Brussels net effective wherever it is used. crosswise of the space to be filled.

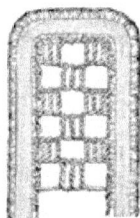

No. 12. POINT DE FILLET (NET GROUNDWORK STITCH).

No. 13.—POINT DE REPRISE.

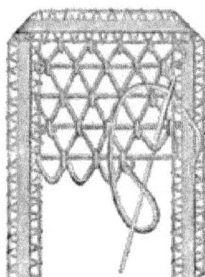

No. 14.—POINT TURQUE (TURKISH STITCH).

making the 3 stitches into the spaces of the nine.

STITCH.—Commence at the

First row.—Work 2 button- the space of 2, work 2, miss the loop and a small one alternately. hole stitches in the larger loops

Third row.—Repeat the first loop of the second row.

OR NET GROUNDWORK STITCH. at No. 21, on page 13, but the here illustrated. It is used for is not imitated, and is very It is begun in the corner or

A loose point de Bruxelles stitch is first taken and fastened to the braid, then passed twice through the braid as shown in the illustration, and worked in rows backward and forward as follows: 1 point de Bruxelles stitch, then before proceeding to the next stitch, pass the needle *under* the knot, *over* the thread, and again *under* it, as shown in the illustration. This stitch is very quickly worked.

No. 13.—POINT DE REPRISE.—This stitch is worked by darning over and under two threads forming a triangle. The space is filled by parallel and crosswise bars placed at equal distances, and on the triangles thus produced point de reprise is worked.

No. 14.—POINT TURQUE, OR TURKISH POINT.—This easy and effective stitch is very appropriate for filling either large or small spaces; the thread employed should be varied in

thickness according space to be filled. a loop into the braid, from right to left, through the twist and engraving), draw up

Second row.—1 right to left. the same as first, us- thread in place of the the needle through vious row, as shown

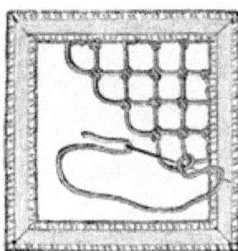

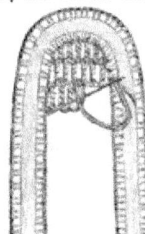

No. 15.—TREBLE POINT D. ESPAGNE.   No. 16.—POINT D'ESPAGNE. (CLOSE.)

(For Directions see Page 12.)

to the size of the

First row.—Work bringing the thread passing the needle through the loop (see tight and repeat. straight thread from

Third row.—Work ing the straight braid, and passing the loop of the pre- in the illustration.

No. 17.—Point de Grecque
(Grecian Point).

No. 18.—Point de Cordova.

No. 15. — Treble Point d' Espagne.—This stitch is worked in exactly the same way as the open and close varieties just mentioned, as follows : 3 close stitches, 1 open, 3 close to the end of each row. Sew back, and in the next row make 1 open, 3 close, 1 open, 3 close to the end; repeat the rows as far as necessary, taking care that the close and open stitches follow in regular order. Diamonds, stars, squares, blocks and various other pretty patterns may be formed with this stitch.

No 16.—Point d'Espagne (Close).—This stitch is worked like open point d'Espagne (see No. 9, page 10) but so closely as to only allow the needle to pass through in the next row. It is also worked from left to right, and is fastened to the braid at the end of each row.

No. 17.—Point de Grecque or Grecian Point.—Point de Grecque is made from left to right, and is worked backward and forward. It is begun by 1 stitch in loose point de Bruxelles and followed by 3 of close point d'Espagne; then 1 Bruxelles, 3 point d'Espagne, to the end of the row; in returning work in the same manner.

No. 18.—Point de Cordova.—This stitch is useful as a variation, and resembles the point de reprise of Guipure lace making. It is worked in a similar manner, over and under the sides of squares formed by intersecting straight lines of the thread.

No. 19.—Point d'Alençon, with Twisted Stitch.—This stitch is used to fill in narrow spaces where great lightness of effect is desired, and is usually seen along the sides of insertions and the tops of edgings. Plain point d'Alençon is worked over and under in bars in a sort of herring-bone pattern, and a twisted stitch is made as seen in the engraving, by twisting the thread three times around each bar and knotting it at the angles as pictured. The effect is similar to one of the drawn-work hem-stitches.

No. 20.—Point d'Angleterre.—This lace is worked as follows : Cover the space to be filled in with lines of thread about an eighth of an inch apart, then form cross-lines, intersecting those already made and passing alternately under and over them ; work a rosette on every spot where two lines cross by working over and under the two lines about 16 times round ; then twist the thread twice round the ground-work thread, and begin to form another rosette at the crossing threads.

No. 21.—Point de Fillet and Point de Reprise.—The net-work seen in this engraving is the first stitch mentioned, while the block-work is the second. Both are clearly illustrated and need no written explanation of the methods employed in making them.

No. 22.—Point de Tulle.—This stitch is used as a ground-work for very fine work, and is worked in rows backward and forward in the same

No. 19.—Point d'Alençon,
with Twisted Thread.

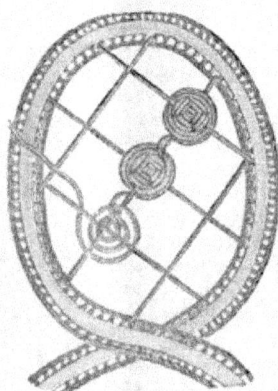

No. 20.—Point d'Angleterre.

stitch as open point d' Espagne. When this is completed the work is gone over a second time by inserting the needle under one twisted bar, bringing it out and inserting it at + and bringing it out again at the dot. This produces a close double twist which is very effective.

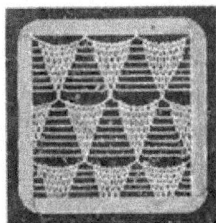

No. 23. FAN LACE STITCH.—Commence at the right side, and work as follows:

First row.—Make 1 button-hole stitch and miss the space of 8, which will leave a long loop.

Second row.—Make 8 button-hole stitches in each loop. *Third row.*—Make 7 stitches into the spaces between the 8, and so decrease one in every row until only one remains, as may be seen by referring to the illustration.

NO. 21.—POINT DE FILLET AND POINT DE REPRISE.

NO. 22.—POINT DE TULLE.

(For directions see Page 12.)

POINT LACE foundation of crossing them to

No. 24.—ROSE STITCH.—Make a single threads, form the large squares. Work a button-hole stitch at each crossing to make it firm. Now begin at the top, at the right side and fill the first square with Brussels net stitches, finishing at the lower left corner. Fill every alternate square in the same way as seen in the picture.

Now cross the open squares diagonally with two threads, twisting each thread around the adjoining one as represented. (Carry one thread across all the squares from corner to corner first, then twist back, fastening at the corner started from; cross these threads in the same way from the opposite direction). When twisting the thread back from the last set of crossings, make a rosette at each center crossing as follows: Keep the space open with a pin and trace round it with a darning movement five or six times; commence at the single thread and work a close button-hole stitch over the tracing entirely around, and then twist along the single thread to the center of the next square. This is a very effective design for spaces.

WHEELS AND ROSETTES.

(For Illustrations see next Page.)

Wheels and rosettes are used to fill up spaces, or in combination, to form lace.

No. 25.—ROSETTE IN RAISED POINT D'ANGLETERRE.—This rosette is worked in a manner similar to the English wheel, the difference being that after each stitch is passed round and under the bars, the thread is passed loosely around in the reverse direction, as shown in the illustration ing to make the

No. 26.—WHEELS.—This is tiest stitches in also one of the work correctly. Work a number of button-hole stitch in one direc- at the opposite way, and work 5 the spot where

No. 23.—FAN LACE STITCH.   No. 24.—ROSE POINT LACE STITCH.

before proceed- next stitch. MECHLIN LACE one of the pret- point lace, but most difficult to It is made thus: diagonal bars in on a single thread tion, then begin side in the same or 6 stitches past the two lines

cross; pass the thread round the cross twice, under and over the thread to form a circle. Work in button-hole stitch half of one-quarter, make a dot by putting a fine pin in the loop instead of drawing the thread tight, and work 3 button-hole stitches in the loop held open by the pin, then take the pin out and continue as before. Beginners will do well to omit the

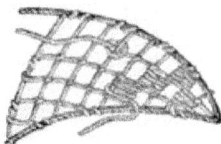

dot, leaving the loop only on the wheel.   Mechlin wheels are also worked in rows upon horizontal and parallel lines of thread.

No. 27.—ENGLISH WHEEL.—This is worked in the same manner as Sorrento wheels, but instead of *winding* the thread over and under the bars, the needle is inserted under each bar, and brought out again between the thread and the last stitch; this produces a kind of button-hole stitch, and gives the square, firm appearance possessed by this wheel.

NOS. 28 AND 30.—SORRENTO WHEEL.—This is worked by fastening the thread in the pattern to be filled up, as indicated by the letters.   Fasten it first to the place *a*, then at place *b*, carrying it back to the middle of the first formed bar by winding it round; fasten again at *c*, carrying it back again to the center by winding it around the bar, and so on to all the letters; then work over and under the bars thus formed.

No. 25.—ROSETTE IN RAISED POINT D'ANGLETERRE.

No. 26.—MECHLIN LACE WHEELS.

No. 27.—ENGLISH WHEEL.

No. 29.—CLOSE ENGLISH be used in open spaces and the engraving. They are much work—indeed, many of the tical with those used in drawn-

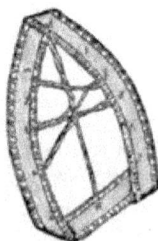

WHEELS.—These wheels may may be very easily made from like the wheels used in drawn stitches used in lace are idenwork.

No. 28.—SORRENTO WHEEL.

No. 29.—CLOSE ENGLISH WHEELS.

No. 30.—SORRENTO WHEEL.

(For Directions for all of the above illustrations see this Page and the preceding one.)

BARS AND PICOTS.

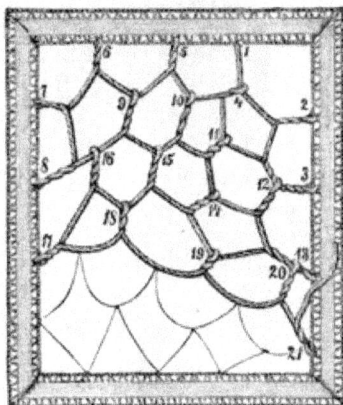

No. 31.—NET-WORK FOR WORKING RALEIGH BARS.

The word "Bar" is applied to the many
stitches used to connect the various parts of
point lace, and the beauty of the work
depends greatly upon the class of bar selected
and its suitability to the lace stitches used.

Nos. 31 AND 32.— RALEIGH BARS.—These
bars are much used in making Battenburg
lace and are very effec- tive. They are worked
over a foundation or net-work of coarse
thread, and are twisted in places so that they
will more easily fall into the desired form.

By following the numbering from 1
to 21, in No. 31, a square place may be
easily filled, and por- tions of this arrangement applied to form ground-work of any
shape desired. Upon this ground-work tight
point de Bruxelles stitches are made, and
the dot worked upon these in one of the
following ways: DOT OR PICOT.—

First Method.—Make 5 tight point de Bruxelles
stitches, 1 loose point de Bruxelles; pass the
needle under the loop and over the thread,
as shown in point de Venise bars at No.
47, on page 18, and draw up, leaving a
small, open loop as in tatting. Work 5 tight
point de Bruxelles stitches, and repeat.

Second Method.—Pro- ceed as above directed,
but instead of continu- ing the tight stitches,
work two or three tight stitches in the loop thus
formed and repeat. *Third Method.*—

Work 4 tight point de Bruxelles stitches; 1
loose, through which pass the needle point,
wind the thread three or four times round the
point (see No. 48, page 18), press the thumb
tightly on this, and draw the needle and thread
through the twists. This is a quick mode of
making the picot, and imitates most closely
the real Spanish lace. Illustration No. 48

shows how this stitch may also be applied as
a *regular* ground-work, but the beauty of old
point ground-work bars consists of variety in
form.

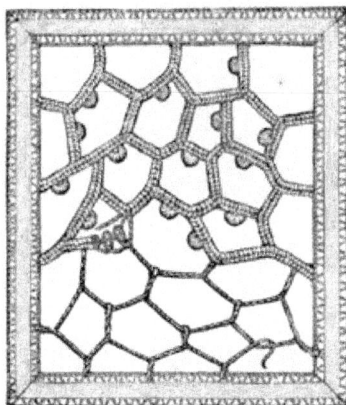

No. 32.—RALEIGH BARS.

No. 33.—ITALIAN GROUND STITCH.

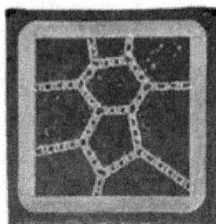

No. 34.—OPEN LACE BARS.

No. 33.—ITALIAN GROUND STITCH.—Commence at the left side, and work as follows:

First row.—Make a loose button-hole stitch to form a loop a quarter of an inch wide, and then make a plain stitch into the loop to twist it, and continue to the end.

Second row.—Make two plain stitches into each loop, working back to the left.

Third row. — Repeat first row.

No. 34.—OPEN LACE BARS.—Pass a thread from right to left. Make it firm by working a second stitch into the braid; work 2 button-hole stitches on this line of thread, close together. Then work 1 button-hole stitch on the lower thread at the left hand side, and draw it close to the 2 stitches on the line of thread. Miss the space of 2 and repeat.

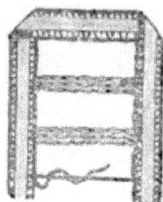

No. 35.—SORRENTO BARS.

No. 36.—SORRENTO BARS.

NOS. 35 AND 36.—SORRENTO BARS.—Each of the bars is worked from right to left, a straight thread being carried across and fastened securely with a stitch. The return consists of a simple twist under and over the straight thread; three of these bars are usually placed close together at equal distances between the groups. The thread is sewn carefully over the braid in passing from one spot to another.

NOS. 37 AND 38.—VENETIAN BARS.—The bar at No. 37 is so simple that it really needs no description. It is worked over two straight threads in reverse button-hole stitch. No. 38 shows the Venetian bar used as the veining of a leaf and worked upon Sorrento bars.

No. 37.—VENETIAN BARS.

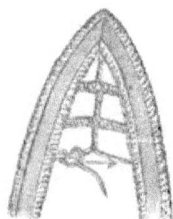

No. 38.—VENETIAN BARS.

No. 39.—POINT D'ANVERS BARS.—Two upright bars form the foundation. The thread is carried over and under them as seen in the engraving, the side loops being added by the method depicted at the top of the point.

The over and under work in point d'Anvers bars, without the side loops, is often used for plain bars for filling in odd spaces or wheels in heavy lace.

No. 40.—POINT GRECQUE BARS.—These bars are so simply made that they are great favorites with beginners. They are begun at the top of the point, one straight thread being carried to the bottom ; then the cross bars are worked after the method seen in the illustration.

No. 39.—POINT D'ANVERS BARS.

No. 40.—POINT GRECQUE BARS.

No. 41.—BARS OF POINT D'ANGLETERRE.—These bars may be worked singly or to fill up a space, as in the illustration. Work rosettes as in point d'Angleterre ; when each rosette is finished twist the thread up the foundation thread to the top, pass it under the parallel center and over into the each side of each rosette, seen in the illustration.

fasten with one stitch, then line running through the opposite braid ; repeat on inserting the threads as

No. 42.—POINT DE Begin at the right hand thread to the left side of one tight stitch of point line work a succession of stitches. Then in every point de Venise stitch.

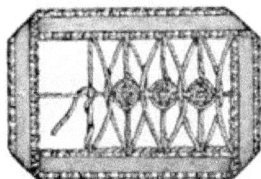

No. 41.—BARS OF POINT D'ANGLETERRE.

VENISE BARS (EDGED).— and stretch a line of the braid, fastening it with de Bruxelles. Upon this tight point de Bruxelles third stitch work one

No. 43.—D'ALENÇON AND SORRENTO BARS.—At Nos. 35 and 36 (page 16), a description of the method of making Sorrento bars is given, while at No. 19 (page 12), is a description of plain and fancy d'Alençon stitches. The two methods are combined in the work seen at No. 43 where the process is so clearly illustrated that a mere novice in lace-work could not fail to produce it perfectly. The combined stitch is used in filling in spaces, etc., etc.

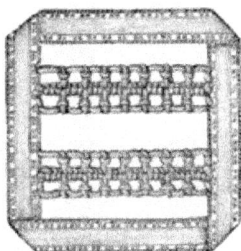

No. 42.—POINT DE VENISE BARS (EDGED).

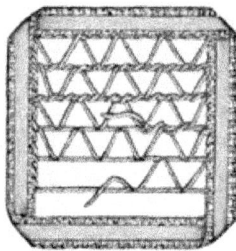

No. 43.—D'ALENÇON AND SORRENTO BARS.

No. 44.—PICOT OR DOT ON SORRENTO BAR.—This dot is worked between rows of point de Bruxelles, 3 twisted stitches being worked into the loop left by the twisted thread; this forms a picot resembling satin stitch in appearance.

No. 45.—D'ALENÇON BARS.—These bars are worked upon point de Bruxelles edging, and are only applied to the inner part of a pattern, never being used as ground-work bars. The thread is merely passed three times over and under the point de Bruxelles stitches, the length of these bars being regulated by the space to be filled; when the third bar is completed a tight point de Bruxelles stitch fastens off the bars, and the thread is passed through the next point de Bruxelles stitch.

No. 46.—PLAIN VENETIAN BARS.—These bars are worked so as to form squares, triangles, etc., in button-hole stitch upon a straight thread.

The *arrow* in the illustration points to the direction for working the next stitch.

No. 44.—PICOT OR DOT ON SORRENTO BAR.

No. 47.—DOTTED POINT DE VENISE BARS.—These pretty bars are worked as follows: Stretch the thread from right to left; on this work 5 tight stitches of point de Bruxelles, then insert a pin in this last stitch to hold it open and loose, pass the needle under the loose stitch and over the thread, as clearly shown in the illustration, and in this loop work 3 tight point de Bruxelles stitches. Then work 5 more stitches and repeat to end of row.

The making of the dots or purls before mentioned as picots, is an important feature in bar work.

No. 45.—D'ALENÇON BARS.   No. 46.—PLAIN VENETIAN BARS.

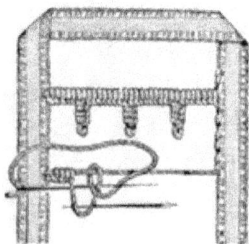

All three names are employed for the same class of stitch.

No. 48.—THIRD METHOD OF MAKING PICOTS OR DOTS.—This method has been fully described in connection with the making of Raleigh Bars at Nos. 31 and 32 (page 15), and requires no further description at this point. All dots and picots render work much more effective, and may be introduced at will by the worker.

In making modern lace, the various kinds require appropriate braids. There are three classes of these braids—those for Battenburg lace, those for plain Honiton and point, and those for the newest kind of lace, which is called the "Ideal Honiton." Each class of braids contains many designs and widths, and a large number of them, together with various cords, buttons and rings also used are illustrated on following pages.

No. 47.—DOTTED POINT DE VENISE BARS.

No. 48.—THIRD METHOD OF MAKING PICOTS OR DOTS.

FANCY BRAIDS, CORDS, RINGS AND BUTTONS.

BRAIDS.

THE braids, cords, rings and buttons illustrated upon the following two pages are all used in modern lace-making. They are all made of pure linen thread, and according to the fancy, the lace including them may be heavy or light. Royal Battenburg lace, as originated, was heavy—in some cases massive; but at present many lighter varieties are made, as will be surmised upon an inspection of the braids for its manufacture which are represented on the pages mentioned. As shown by No. 1, these braids are about a third narrower than their actual width, and the picot edges numbered 16 and 17 are plain tatting made for the purpose, as the picot edges woven for lighter laces are not heavy enough for Battenburg lace. The numbers opposite the specimens are simply for convenience in ordering, if the order is sent the lady mentioned in another part of the book as the Pioneer of Lace-Making in America; but in ordering from other lace-makers or manufacturers of braids, these numbers will be of little use, as every lace-maker or manufacturer has his or her own individual identifications for materials. Almost any of the braids, or those very similar, may be found at large fancy stores, but in buying them at such stores, be careful to get *linen* braids, as cotton braids do not make pretty lace, neither do they wear or launder well. In ordering these braids from other lace-makers or from fancy stores, it will be necessary to forward the illustration of the kind wanted, as the braids cannot be described with sufficient accuracy to obtain the desired varieties. Some are sold by the yard, some by the dozen yards and others by the piece, according to the position to be occupied in the work.

The point, Honiton and Princess braids are represented full size, and are much daintier in texture than the Battenburg braids. Of this class of braids (see No. 2) are made the plain Honiton and point laces, and the braids for these two laces combined produce the Princess lace—a creation whose beauty fully entitles it to its royal name.

The braids seen at No. 3, page 21, are those which are used in making the new "Ideal Honiton" lace represented in another portion of the book. As illustrated, these braids are three-quarters of their proper widths, the top braid, No. 38, being just one inch wide in the fabric itself. The "Ideal Honiton" is one of the prettiest laces made, and is very appropriate for tidies, doilies, squares and scarfs. It is daintily secured to the finest of lawn in charming designs, and then the lawn is cut out from beneath it. (See doily, page 33).

The cords seen at No. 4 are used in making Battenburg laces, and greatly increase the beauty of the work in addition to forming a distinctive species of lace. After the ordinary Battenburg is worked with quite thick braid, the cord, in any size desired, is used to follow one edge of the design, as will be seen from illustrations upon other following pages.

RINGS AND BUTTONS.

The rings and buttons illustrated, are made throughout of linen thread in layers of buttonhole stitches, and are sold by the dozen or gross. Buttons arranged as grapes (see No. 50, page 21), add greatly to the sumptuous effect of a heavy lace, and may be purchased already arranged as illustrated, or they may be arranged by the purchaser of a quantity of them. The latter method is a good plan if spaces are to be filled with clusters which must be of a certain shape.

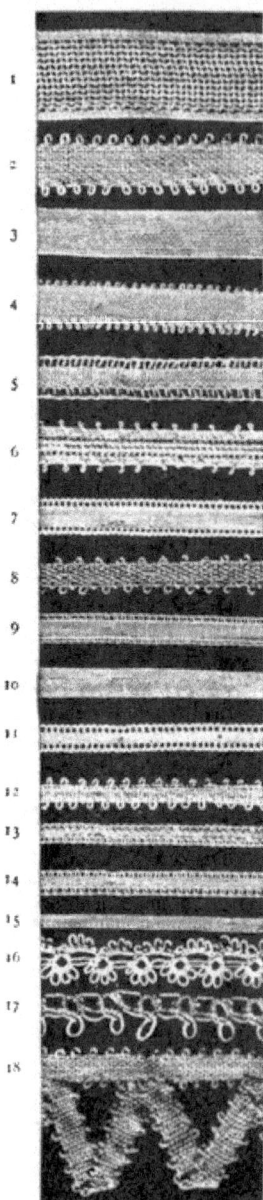

No. 1.—Braids used in Making Battenburg Lace.   No. 2.—Braids used in Making Honiton, Point
                                                           and Princess Lace.

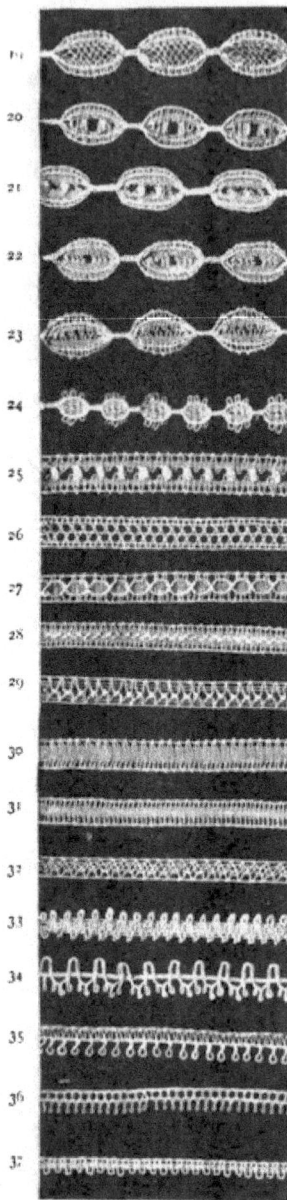

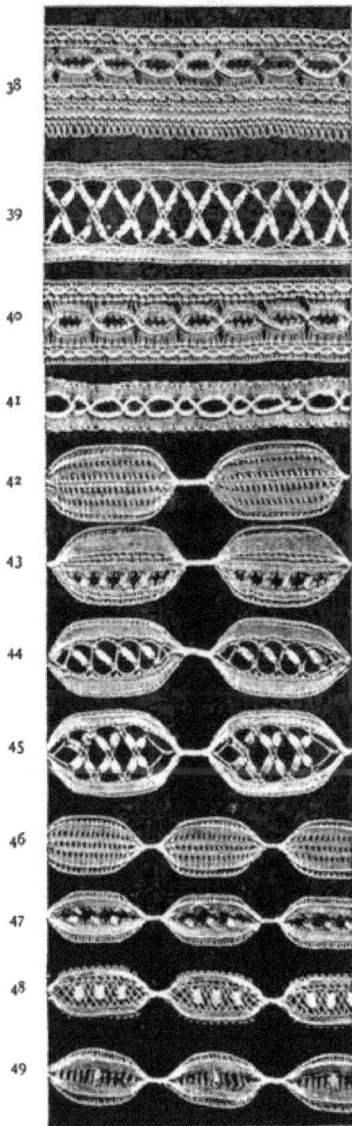

No. 3.—Braids used in Making "Ideal Honiton"
Lace.

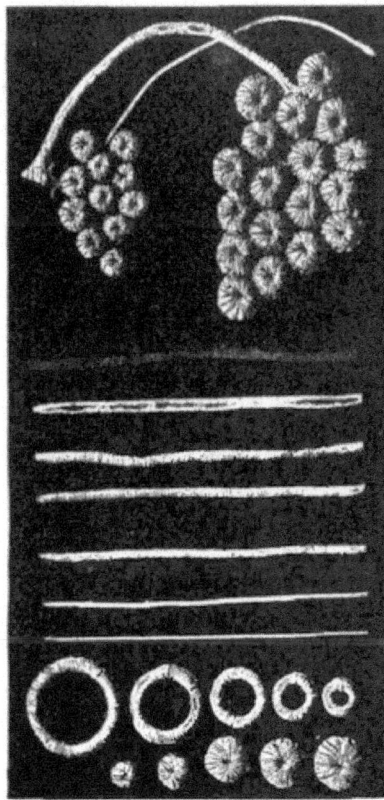

No. 4.—Cords, Rings and Buttons used in Making Battenburg Lace.

DESIGNS, LACE ARTICLES, EDGINGS, INSERTIONS, ETC., IN MODERN LACE.

Of necessity, most of the designs and specimens given on this and the following pages are smaller than the articles they represent, but they afford a correct idea of the method of making and the beauty of, Modern Lace, and also its adaptability to dainty accessories of the toilet and the household. As before mentioned any design desired can be obtained from any lace-making establishment in any size, width or shape, according to the requirements of the article or lace to be made, and individual taste. Ingenious students will no doubt be able to adapt for themselves the designs offered, but it is not advisable for those who have no talent in the matter of drawing or designing to undertake an elaborate adaptation, though they may easily accomplish a simple one. Besides, a professional designer will furnish the design for a moderate sum, perfectly outlined upon tracing cloth, with ink, and with the proper filling-in stitches perfectly delineated; and if the student wishes it, will select the thread and braid appropriate for the design; or the student may select the braid she fancies, and the designer will then select the thread suitable for the braid.

No. 1.
DESIGN FOR A LACE HANDKERCHIEF.

This design is suitable for point lace braid, but is of course very much reduced in size, in order to show the effect and arrangement of a design ready for working, as sent out from the lace-maker's. By a reference to the various stitches illustrated on preceding pages, the stitches shown in one corner of the design may be readily identified. The following engraving shows how braid is applied to a design before the stitches are begun.

No. 2.
METHOD OF PLACING BRAID UPON DESIGNS.

This illustration shows the method of arranging braid upon designs for modern lace, and how, after the braid is basted along the pattern, the tracing cloth is basted to *toile cirée* or to smooth, light brown wrapping paper to provide sufficient firmness for working.

The following instructions apply particularly to engraving No. 2, but their principle should be observed and applied to any design decided upon, as good results in lace-making largely depend upon the arrangement of the braid.

Run on a straight line of braid for the lower edge, with fine stitches, working as shown, from left to right. Take another piece of braid, or the other end of the same piece, and begin to lay the braid by "running" stitches in its center, keeping it as smooth and even as possible. The outer edge presents no difficulty, but the inner edge will not lie evenly without being drawn in by a needle and thread, as follows: Fasten whipping thread securely, and insert the needle in and out of the edge of the braid, as if for fine gathering; this thread when drawn up will keep the braid in its place. Two or three fastening-off stitches should be worked when each circle, half circle, or rounded curve of a pattern is finished, as the drawing or gathering thread remains in the work, and forms an important, though unseen, part of its structure.

Before cutting off the braid run a few stitches across it to prevent it from widening. Joins should be avoided, but when a join is indispensable, stitch the braid together, open and turn back the ends, and stitch each portion down separately. When passing the thread from one part to another, run it along the center of the braid, allowing the stitches to show as little as possible. In commencing, make a few stitches, leaving the end of the thread on the wrong side and cutting it off afterwards. In fastening off, make a tight button-hole stitch, run in three stitches, bring the needle out at the back, and cut off.

No. 1.—Design for a Lace Handkerchief.

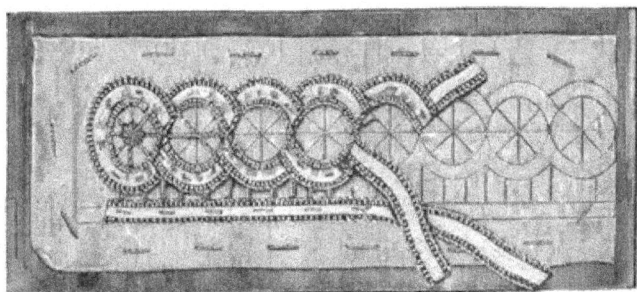

No. 2.—Method of Placing Braid upon Designs.

No. 3.

ROYAL BATTENBURG LACE BUREAU-SCARF.

The engraving on the opposite page represents the article above mentioned, and shows the effectiveness of this magnificent and durable lace. In actual size the scarf is about a yard and one-half long and one-half yard wide, and is made of a heavy Battenburg braid, having a fancy edge (See Nos. 5 or 7, on page 20) and cord, rings and buttons. The main part of the design is outlined with the braid, cord is used as a veining for the leaves, and the rings and buttons are introduced here and there over the surface, as seen in the picture. Raleigh bars with picots connect the border and center designs, while the palms along the border as well as other small spaces are filled in with point Turque and point de Grecque stitches. Sorrento bars are also used in some of the long leaf-like spaces, while in a few of the circular spaces point d'Angleterre rosettes are introduced. These rosettes are also frequently called "spiders," and are made, according to the space, large or small; and according to the requirements of the braid selected, heavy or light.

For convenience in giving the name of this lace, the full title is rarely used—" Battenburg Lace " being considered sufficient to identify the fabric from the other and lighter laces.

Battenburg lace is made both heavy and light, according to personal taste or the object for which the lace is intended, but it was originally designed for heavy work only.

No. 3.—ROYAL BATTENBURG LACE BUREAU-SCARF.

No. 4.

POINT LACE DOILY FOR A TOILET CUSHION.

This dainty doily may be made of the point lace braids illustrated at Nos. 30 and 31, to-gether with the picot edging No. 36, seen on page 20.   In filling in the spaces, thread suitable for the braid is used, and the stitches are point de Valenciennes, point d'Espagne, Sorrento bars, point de Bruxelles, open rings and "spiders."   As all of these stitches, with many others are illustrated in that section of this book devoted to stitches, it will be unnecessary to repeat the details for making, as they are fully given in the department mentioned.   It will also be understood that most of the articles illustrated are not of full size, but in some instances are nearly so.   The doily just described is illustrated about three-quarters of its actual size ; but by using a fine braid a doily of fairy-like texture, and just the size of the engraving may be produced.   Any one accustomed to drawing may enlarge this or any of the designs given, but only clever fingers should try this experiment.

No. 4.—Point Lace Doily for a Toilet Cushion.

No. 5.

BATTENBURG EDGING, WITH CORD.

This is a very elegant looking lace, though simply made after the regular Battenburg method. A plain braid (No. 10, page 20) is chosen to form the outlines, and after the stitches are filled in, cord of a suitable size is carried around the petals and foliage of the design, and rows of it are also used to indicate the vine, though the latter may be outlined with the tape and then with the cord. The petals of the blossoms are filled in in point de Bruxelles and point de Venise stitches, while point d'Espagne and point Brabançon are used for the foliage and vine. Point Grecque and d'Alençon bars are also used at the very heart of the blossom, and Raleigh net-work bars connect the design to the edge and are dotted here and there with " spiders."

No. 6.

BATTENBURG INSERTION, WITH CORD.

This insertion matches the edging or lace above described, and is, therefore, made in exactly the same way, except that the design is double. Both the edging and insertion may be made of any width desired ; and the design will be found very pretty for fancy-edge or plain braids without the cord. Buttons or rings may be used in place of the " spiders " seen in the engravings if preferred.

No. 5.—BATTENBURG LACE, WITH CORD.

No. 6.—BATTENBURG INSERTION, WITH CORD.

No. 7.

DESIGN FOR A HONITON LACE CAP.

The design illustrated is, of necessity, much smaller than the cap it is intended for; but the clever student may easily enlarge it to, or design one for herself of the size required. Lace-makers will duplicate designs in any size desired for a moderate sum, thus saving the amateur much work and at the same time putting her to little expense.

The design here illustrated might also be used for handkerchief corners, scarf-ends, etc., etc.; and any of the stitches illustrated on preceding pages may be selected for filling-in purposes.

No. 8.

DESIGN FOR A CORNER IN BATTENBURG, POINT, OR HONITON LACE.

According to the article to be decorated, this design will be found appropriate for either of the braids used for the laces above mentioned.

For table scarfs, tidies, heavy borders, etc., etc., the Battenburg braids should be selected; but for handkerchiefs or doilies, the point or Honiton braids are the proper ones to choose for this design.

Raleigh bars, Brussels point and any other stitches preferred, may be used in filling in the spaces. When a design is procured from a lace-maker a portion of it is always marked with the stitches to be used; but this is not an arbitrary matter, since the one who is to make the lace, may desire to and may insert other stitches in preference to those indicated.

No. 7.—DESIGN FOR A HONITON LACE CAP.

No. 8.—DESIGN FOR A CORNER IN BATTENBURG, POINT, OR HONITON LACE.

No. 9.

DOILY IN "IDEAL HONITON" LACE-WORK AND LINEN LAWN.

One of the prettiest and the very newest of the modern laces is here illustrated. It is made of two of the many varieties of Honiton braids, wash-silk floss and linen lawn. The braid is basted smoothly upon a square of lawn in the design illustrated (though individual taste will no doubt suggest many other equally pretty designs), after which the *inner* edges of the braid are permanently secured by a "short and long stitch." This is merely a short and long button-hole stitch *reversed* so that the cross loops are on the edge of the braid, while the stitches them selves extend beyond the braid, into the lawn, as seen in the engraving. Two short stitches alternate with single long ones throughout this part of the work. The outer edges are then fastened to the square by tiny button-hole scollops. Then the lawn is cut from under the squares formed by the braid, and the openings are button-holed through the lawn and braid so that the edges of the lawn will not fray. When this is done the spaces are filled in with fancy stitches, and when they are completed the lawn is cut away from the edge-scollops with a pair of fine sharp scissors. In the doily illustrated "spiders" and point de Venise stitches are used for filling in the spaces. The floss used may be white or tinted, the latter washing as well as the white ; but as a rule, white or yellow flosses are selected in preference to other colors. "Ideal Honiton" scarfs, tidies, doilies, pillow shams, tray cloths, etc., etc., may be purchased with the braid already basted on in a pretty design and with the necessary threads or floss, or they may be designed at home, and by either method will result in a beautiful variety of modern lace.

No. 9.—DOILY OF "IDEAL HONITON" LACE AND LINEN LAWN.

No. 10.

DESIGN FOR A CORNER IN BATTENBURG LACE.

Although this design is intended for Battenburg lace, and may be made up of any of the braids used for that kind of lace, it will also be found suitable for the finer point or Honiton braids for handkerchiefs, doilies, mats, etc., etc. As illustrated it would be suitable for a handkerchief. Enlarged and followed in Battenburg braid it would make a very handsome border for a table-scarf, curtains or draperies, or a substantial decoration for a gown of wash fabric or other goods. Raleigh bars, "spiders" and point de Bruxelles stitches are used for filling in, and a dainty picot edge is sewed to the outer line of the braid. Plain or fancy braid may be used for this design. If fancy loop-edge braid is selected, the picot edge will not be needed, the loops taking its place.

No. 10.—Design for a Corner in Battenburg Lace.

No. 11.

BATTENBURG EDGING.

The edging here illustrated is represented about one-third less than its actual width, but the design is so distinctly brought out that its beauty in any width may be readily conceived. It is formed of fancy Battenburg braid, but may be made from a plain variety if preferred. The design is known as the fern leaf and is easy to follow. Sorrento bars are used to connect the work, and "spiders" are made here and there to add variety to the work. Point de Bruxelles stitches are used to fill in the spaces at the sides of the leaves, and, with the fancy braid, produce a very dainty, delicate effect.

No. 12.

BATTENBURG INSERTION.

This insertion is made to match the edging seen above it, but is much wider than the edging, though formed of the same braid. Either design could be varied so as to result in an edging and insertion of equal width, or the edging could be arranged for an insertion, and the insertion illustrated changed into an edging.

No. 11.—BATTENBURG EDGING.

No. 12.—BATTENBURG INSERTION.

No. 13.

FINGER-BOWL DOILY OF PRINCESS LACE AND LINEN LAWN.

Princess lace, (also known as Duchesse lace) as elsewhere mentioned, results from combining Honiton and point lace braids in one design; and a charming specimen of this lovely lace is here illustrated.

The doily is pictured only a trifle smaller than its actual size, and even in its full size is a very dainty affair. After the braids are basted along the design, they are then connected by twisted bars that are an adaptation from the point d'Alençon bars with the twisted stitch; and the spaces are filled in in small d'Angleterre rosettes or "spiders." As few bars as possible are employed for the spiders, in order to produce a very delicate effect. The lawn center is added last.

No. 13.—Finger-Bowl Doily of Princess Lace and Linen Lawn.

No. 14.

DESIGN FOR INSERTION, OR A CENTER-PIECE, IN BATTENBURG LACE.

As suggested by the title, the design here presented may beused for insertion, or for a center to a table cloth or scarf, or a handsome spread. As represented it is intended for a center-piece, and the lace from which the engraving was made is about half-a-yard long and one-fourth of a yard wide. The ground-work is formed of Raleigh bars made with picots, and the loops of braid are filled in with twisted point d'Alençon bars.

This center-piece is very pretty made of ribbon with silk thread for the bars, and in this event it may be made of any color desired, and added to a spread or scarf of surah silk or fine cloth, for which a border to match may be mad

No. 15.

QUEEN ANNE TRAY-CLOTH OF BATTENBURG LACE AND LINEN.

This pretty cloth is intended for a Queen Anne tray, and its lace edges curve upward and just over the rim of the tray when it is laid upon it. The center is of fine table-linen, while the edge is formed of Battenburg braid, buttons and fancy stitches. As will be seen, the corner spaces are filled in with point d'Angleterre rosettes or "spiders," the large border spaces and corresponding corner ones are filled in with picot bars, while the very fine work seen in the triangles and square spaces are point de Venise stitches, and half-spiders are made in the other triangles. The narrow, straight inner border is composed of bars and tiny buttons arranged as represented. The cloth is hem-stitched before the braid is laid on, and the corners are cut out from underneath after the work is otherwise completed.

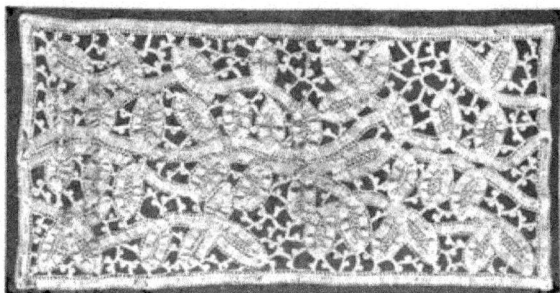

No. 14.—DESIGN FOR INSERTION, OR A CENTER-PIECE, IN BATTENBURG LACE.

No. 15.—QUEEN ANNE TRAY-CLOTH OF BATTENBURG LACE AND LINEN.

No. 16.

DESIGN FOR A BUTTERFLY IN POINT LACE. (FULL SIZE).

Butterflies for the corners of handkerchiefs, scarf-ends and the points of caps or coiffures are favorite designs in point and Honiton laces. The one illustrated is very dainty and exceedingly simple to execute. The upper portion of each wing has a point de reprise groundwork, but the solid sections are tiny spiders instead of point de reprise triangles. The outer tips of the wings are filled in with Raleigh bars, while similar bars, point de Bruxelles stitches and a point d'Angleterre rosette complete the lower wings. Any of the fine point or Honiton braids may be chosen for the outlining of the butterfly, and a fine over-and-over stitch or fine cord may be used to mark the lines extending from the head.

No. 17.

DESIGN FOR A DOILY OR HANDKERCHIEF OF POINT OR HONITON LACE.

This design, as illustrated, is of course too small for either a doily or handkerchief, but an expert lace-maker can enlarge it to any size desired; and the clever amateur will find no difficulty in doing the same thing, as the outlines are not at all intricate, and may be easily followed. In sending for the braid for this, or similar designs, it is advisable to permit the lace-maker addressed to select them, and of course, the thread, since her long experience enables her at once to correctly judge what materials are appropiate for the articles you wish to make, especially if she knows the size the article is desired to be. The stitches, as here indicated, are point d'Angleterre rosettes, and point de fillet, with small "spiders" on the latter. A dainty picot-braid edges the design.

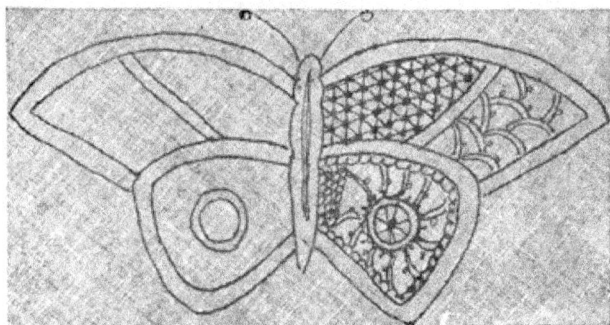

No. 16.—Design for a Butterfly in Point Lace. (Full Size).

No. 17.—Design for a Doily or Handkerchief of Point or Honiton Lace. (Half Size.)

No. 18.

"CARDINAL'S POINT" LACE.

This engraving represents a modern adaptation of an ancient lace which may be made of fancy Battenburg braid and plain Raleigh bars. The design is not especially definite in its outlines, and may be imitated with any variations which may seem pleasing to the copyist. The picots are made after the method directed at the illustration of point de Venise bars in the department devoted to stitches. "Cardinal's point" of genuine make is of Italian origin, and in the earlier eras, was largely used for the decoration of church vestments and draperies.

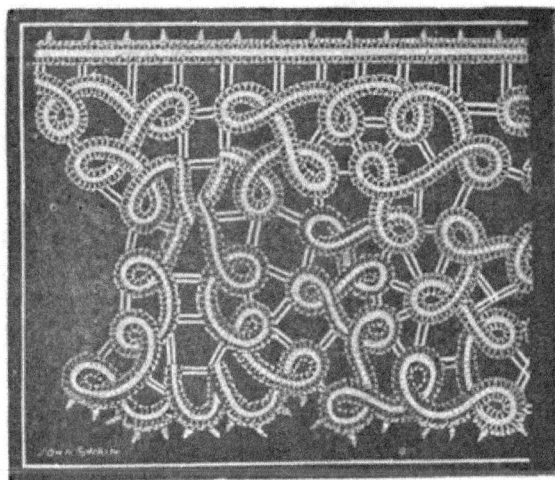

No. 18   "Cardinal's Point" Lace.

Nos. 19 and 20.

BATTENBURG EDGING AND INSERTION, WITH CORD.

These two engravings show a very pretty design for Battenburg lace made with a cord finish. The application of the cord has been fully described elsewhere, where a different design of the same kind of work is given. In the present instance the spaces are filled in with twisted bars, "spiders" and rosettes in point d'Angleterre. The specimens from which the engravings were made are a trifle wider than seen in the pictures; but the width is a matter of individual taste, and also a result of the braid selected. A professional lace-maker will enlarge or adapt the design to accord with personal requirements.

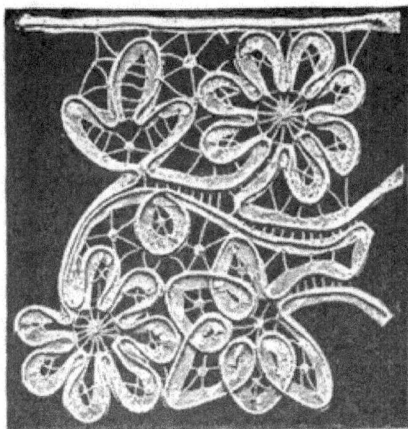

No. 19.—BATTENBURG EDGING, WITH CORD.

No. 20.—BATTENBURG INSERTION, WITH CORD.

No. 21.

TAPE-GUIPURE DESIGN, FOUND IN AN OLD CHURCH.

The design here illustrated was found in the old church of Santa Margherita, in Italy. It was drawn on parchment, and was undoubtedly intended as a design for altar lace. It was mentioned in a book of accounts for the year 1592, found in the archives of the church designated and is therefore of antique origin; but it may be easily adapted to modern methods of lace-making, and could be appropriately filled in with either Italian or Genoa lace stitches or with a combination of both, and twisted bars. Done with fancy Battenburg braid, it would be quite similar in effect to the "Cardinal's Point" illustrated on another page.

No. 21.—TAPE-GUIPURE DESIGN, FOUND IN AN OLD CHURCH.

No. 22.

BATTENBURG CHURCH LACE.

The engraving opposite illustrates a magnificent specimen of Modern Church Lace made of Battenburg braid with a limited introduction of Honiton braid. The specimen itself is considerably wider than represented, but as the width is a matter of individual taste, the engraving will serve as a design for a narrow church lace.

Sorrento bars are used to connect the braids and to form foundations for the spiders or rosettes here and there inserted, and the lace is delicately bordered with a dainty picot-braid. The fancy stitches in the main portions of the cross are point de Valenciennes, while those in the minor sections are point de Bruxelles.

Point de fillet is used for the central portion of the large T-shaped symbol, while the stitch forming the other symbol is one never used except for church lace, and consists of two or three sets of fine stitches so interlaced as to seem to form one solid stitch.

In making church lace any insignia desired can be introduced by a professional designer—an accomplishment that is usually beyond the inventive powers of the novice in lace-making.

No. 22.—BATTENBURG CHURCH LACE.

No. 23.

ENGLISH NEEDLE-POINT.

This is a very handsome design combining the lily and the rose. The foundation work is made with unbleached linen braid having an ornamental edge, and the filling-in is done with fine and coarse linen thread in various stitches. Raleigh bars with picots define the upper edge of the edging, and Sorrento bars on which buttons are worked form the ground work.

Point de Grecque, point d'Angleterre, d'Alençon bars plain and twisted, point de Bruxelles and "spiders" are also used in making this lace, as will be seen from a close inspection of the engraving.

This specimen of lace is very handsome when developed in black silk braids and silk thread, for black costumes.

No. 23.—ENGLISH NEEDLE POINT.

No. 24.

PUNCH-GLASS DOILY OF POINT LACE AND LAWN.

As represented this doily is about three-fourths of its actual size. It is made of fine linen lawn, and a set generally comprises a dozen. Fine point lace braid is used to outline the design, and then rosettes in point d'Angleterre, and "spiders" or small rosettes are made in the openings as represented. The alternate outer scallops are filled in with point de Bruxelles stitches, and a dainty picot-braid is added to the edge by the usual over-and-over stitch.

No. 25.

POINT LACE COLLAR AND CUFF.

A very handsome point lace set is here illustrated, and may be easily followed by an expert lace-maker; but it will be wiser for the novice to obtain a pattern or design of the shape and size desired, from a professional lace-maker. Point de Grecque, point de Bruxelles, point de Venise, Sorrento bars, and rosettes and rings are all employed in carrying out this design. As elsewhere mentioned, any fine stitch preferred may be used for filling in purposes when those suggested or marked out upon a design are not admired.

No. 24.—Punch-Glass Doily of Point Lace and Lawn.

No. 25.—Point Lace Collar and Cuff.

No. 26.

DESIGN FOR TABLE SCARF IN BATTENBURG LACE.

The scarf-end from which this design was copied is about ten inches deep, and it is about fourteen or fifteen inches wide. It will be seen from these dimensions, that it is impossible to produce a full-size design of it on these pages, but one of any size desired may be obtained at any lace-makers; or, a clever student of lace-making may enlarge the design to suit her own requirements. According to the size of the scarf-end, wide or narrow braid must be selected, with thread to correspond. The stitches used in filling in are point de fillet, point de Bruxelles and point d'Angleterre, and Raleigh, Sorrento and d'Alençon bars, and rosettes and "spiders."

No. 27.

APPLE DESIGN FOR A CORNER IN BATTENBURG LACE.

This design is for the corner of a scarf, spread, tidy or pillow-sham and is very popular, as it is effective though simply made. The fine stitches are point de Bruxelles, while the others are Raleigh, Sorrento and point Grecque bars. Plain or fancy braid, or a combination of both may be used in this design with a charming effect.

No. 26.—Design for a Table Scarf in Battenburg Lace.

No. 27.—Apple Design for a Corner in Battenburg Lace.

No. 28.

ROMAN PUNCH-GLASS DOILY IN POINT LACE.

Doilies of this description are generally made about four inches square. The engraving opposite pictures the doily mentioned as somewhat smaller, but the design is sufficiently large to enable the student to make her doilies as large as she desires them to be, as it easy to follow. The corner spaces are filled in with twisted bars and rings worked at the same time ; but rosettes or spiders may be worked in place of the rings if preferred. The corner spaces are filled in in point Brabançon, and for those at each side point de Bruxelles is used. The doily is edged with a fine picot-braid that finishes it daintily, and very sheer linen lawn is used for the center.

No. 29.

MODERN RUSSIAN LACE.

The design illustrated may be followed in Battenburg braid or plain lace tape, and any of the fancy stitches mentioned and described among the rosettes, bars and picots may be employed for filling-in purposes. Cream white or unbleached braids or tapes are prettier for Russian lace than pure white. Russian lace is a very durable as well as effective trimming for household draperies, and also for gowns of wash fabrics or those of cotton fabrics which will not need renovating.

No. 28.—Roman Punch-Glass Doily in Point Lace.

No. 29.—Modern Russian Lace.

No. 30.

RUSSIAN LACE.

This engraving represents a specimen of genuine Russian lace made of fine braid, and wrought with bars similar to Raleigh bars, except that they have no picots. The Russians have always been noted for their exquisite needle-work, but as a nation they have never had any established lace manufactory. The workers of the small amount of lace produced are scattered about at their own houses, and many of them are poor ladies of gentle birth. Most of the laces, however, are made by the peasantry, who bring them to St. Petersburg where sale for them is found.

No. 30.—RUSSIAN LACE.

BOW-KNOT DESIGN FOR MODERN LACE.

This fashionable design may be developed in various widths and braids as an insertion, or as an appliqué on lawn. The ground-work may be formed of Raleigh bars, or of twisted bars made like the net-work for Raleigh bars. The loops of the bows may be filled in with point de Bruxelles or any fine stitch preferred. The design is pretty for bordering table scarfs, tidies, valances and curtains when heavy braids are selected. The finer braids render the design appropriate for handkerchiefs and dainty trimming laces.

No. 32.

PRINCESS LACE DOILY DESIGN.

The design here illustrated may be enlarged or simplified to please individual taste, and it may be made of Honiton braid as well as point. The connecting stitches may be point de Bruxelles, Raleigh and Sorrento bars, "spiders" or any of the fine stitches described and illustrated in the department devoted to stitches. A dainty picot braid follows the outer edge of the doily. This design, enlarged sufficiently, would form an elegant pattern for a lace handkerchief.

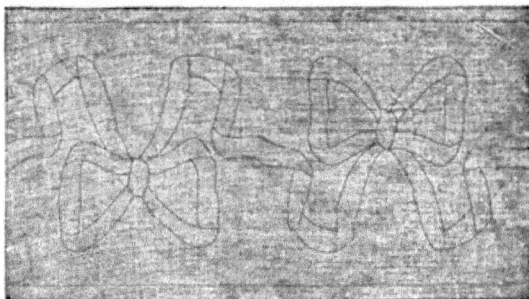

No. 31.—Bow-Knot Design for Modern Lace.

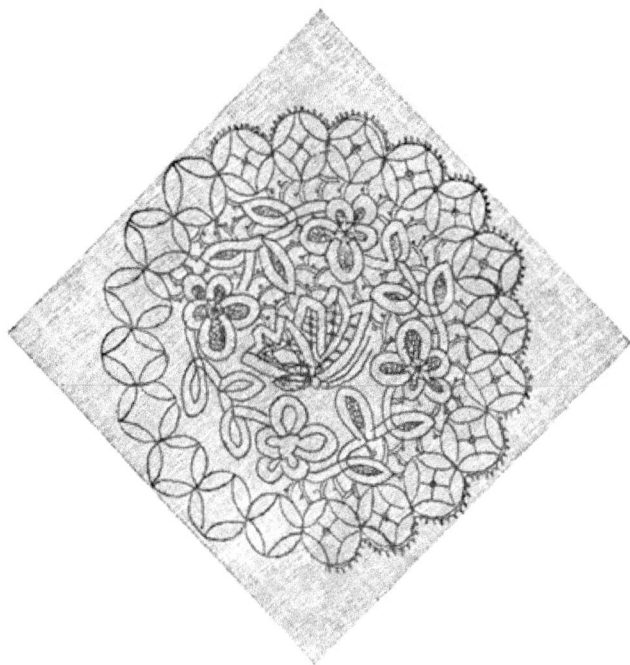

No. 32.—Princess Lace Doily Design.

No. 35.

ALTAR LACE (BATTENBURG).

This very elegant specimen of altar lace is, in reality, about nine or ten inches deep; but, for want of space the engraving represents it as only about half as wide. The design, however, is perfect in detail, and the illustration fully displays its effectiveness, and discloses the variety of connecting and filling-in stitches used. A delicate Battenburg braid is chosen for the foundation, and in addition to regular lace stitches, those from drawn work are here and there interspersed. The cross is filled in in point de Venise, (or side stitch as it is sometimes called), and the same stitch is seen in the central design at each side of the cross. Drawn-work effects are seen also in these central figures and along the borders. Sorrento bars are here made and knotted at the center like drawn strands, or are connected by rosettes or "spiders" made in drawn-work style. At the center of the cross is a large drawn-work wheel, while small Maltese crosses and half-crosses are made elsewhere in the work by the drawn-work method, Sorrento bars taking the place of the usual strands. The central section of the border at the right of the cross is done in point de Bruxelles which is afterward button-holed as in bar-work, and a button-hole picot edge follows the lower outlines of the pattern. Raleigh bars with picots form the connecting ground-work throughout the work. This beautiful specimen shows two distinct methods of filling in the sections between the crosses. Either may be used alone, or the two may be used alternately with the crosses.

No. 33.—ALTAR LACE (BATTENBURG.)

No. 34.

BATTENBURG OR POINT LACE COLLAR AND CUFF.

These engravings represent a very graceful design for a lace collar and cuffs. As suggested in the title, the set may be made of point or Battenburg braid. The leaf-points are all filled in with d'Alençon bars in the twisted stitch, while the centers are completed with rosettes or small open "spiders," and the latter are distributed elsewhere as will be seen by inspecting the engraving. Point de Grecque is also introduced into some of the spaces, and Raleigh bars are used for the ground-work. Any of the stitches previously described may be used in making such a collar if those mentioned are not admired; and the addition of buttons or rings will improve the work greatly.

No. 34.—BATTENBURG OR POINT LACE COLLAR AND CUFF.

No. 35.

FLOUNCE IN BATTENBURG LACE.

A very elegant flounce of Battenburg lace may be made after the design represented on the opposite page. The picture shows the flounce just one-half its actual width; but even this width would be very handsome as a band for the bottom of a dress. By a close inspection of the stitches seen and a reference to these illustrated in the department devoted to stitches, the various kinds here used may be easily identified. They consist of point de Venise, point de Bruxelles, Sorrento and Alençon bars and "spiders." A fine picot braid edges each side of the flounce. The design can be obtained in any width desired from a reliable lace-maker.

No. 35.—FLOUNCE IN BATTENBURG LACE (ONE-HALF THE ACTUAL WIDTH).

No. 36.

BUTTERFLY DESIGN FOR POINT LACE.

This design is for point lace braid, and is very easily made. Fancy bars made after an adaptation from the d'Alençon bars, and point de Venise stitches are used for filling in. The butterfly may be used as a portion of an edging design, or as a corner or center for any small article to be decorated. The lines extending from the head are made with a fine over-and-over stitch, or a fine cord.

No. 37.

VENETIAN POINT LACE.

This is a design containing many of the features of antique lace patterns, and is made of narrow tape and fine cord combined with fancy stitches. The lace from which the engraving is made is about twice as wide as the picture represents it, but as the pattern differs in its sections for several inches at a time, the design could not be given full size. It will be seen that in the section illustrated no two figures are alike. The filling-in stitches consist of combinations and groupings of many of the stitches previously illustrated and described.

No. 38.

BUTTERFLY DESIGN FOR FINE BATTENBURG LACE.

This design, developed in Battenburg lace with d'Alençon and Sorrento bars and small "spiders" or dots, makes a pretty ornament for centers or corners, or is effective when introduced as a part of an edging design. Point or Honiton braids may also be made up by this design.

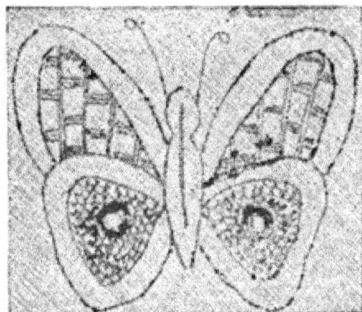

No. 36.—Butterfly Design for Point Lace.

No. 37.—Venetian Point Lace.

No. 38.—Butterfly Design for fine Battenburg Lace.

No. 39.

DESIGN FOR INSERTION.

A very pretty design for insertion is here given. The braid may be basted as seen in the picture, and then the bars may be made of single threads, and of single threads overwrought with button-hole stitches. Or, any of the bars or other stitches described, may be used to connect the braid and fill in the spaces. Tiny "spiders" are already used to fill in the circles.

No. 40.

DESIGN FOR A LACE BORDER AND CORNER.

A great deal must be left to the ingenuity of the worker in filling in this design, which is not of the orthodox modern variety but may be readily transformed into that class by an adaptation of modern stitches. With the methods of the latter well mastered, the worker will have no trouble in bringing out the design just as it is illustrated; but she may also by the exercise of a little judgment and taste substitute many other pretty filling-in stitches for those here pictured.

No. 39.—Design for Insertion.

No. 40.—Design for a Lace Border and Corner.

No. 41.

DESIGN FOR A BUTTERFLY IN POINT LACE.

Another butterfly design is here given for point lace, though it may also be developed in in a larger size in Battenburg braid for decorative purposes. The filling-in stitches are d'Alençon and Raleigh bars, point de Venise and point de Bruxelles, and point d'Angleterre rosettes.

No. 42.

ITALIAN LACE.

This lace is of a conventional Italian pattern, and is filled in with the Italian lace and ground-stitches, and Sorrento bars. The lower edge is very daintily completed with a button-hole effect. The design is simple, elegant, and popular, and may be wrought in Battenburg or the finer braids, and in any width desired, the braid selected and the width decided upon determining the use to which the lace shall be put.

No. 41.—Design for a Butterfly in Point Lace.

No. 42.—Italian Lace (Half Size).

No. 43.

MODERN VENETIAN POINT.

The engraving shows a reduced representation of a very elegant specimen of modern lace—the reduction in size being necessary in order to present the whole design. In making the lace, narrow braid and cord are used for the foundation of the design, and then the filling-in stitches are made and at the same time rings and buttons and bars and picots are introduced. Some of the filling-in stitches are combinations—as in the figures with very open bars where point d'Espagne and point Brabançon are combined, and at the middle section of the central figure where point de Valenciennes and point Brabançon are combined. Other stitches used are d'Alençon bars, Raleigh bars, church stitch, point de Bruxelles, "spiders," Sorrento bars, and picots. The greater the variety in the filling-in stitches, the more beautiful the lace. A picot edge finishes the lace in a very dainty manner along its lower outline, while a cord forms the upper edge.

No. 43.—MODERN VENETIAN POINT.

No. 45.

DESIGN FOR MODERN LACE.

This design may be made up in Battenburg braid, or of point or Honiton braid according to the texture of the lace desired.   In making it for garments or articles that are to be renovated occasionally, the Battenburg braids are advisable ; but for daintier uses, point or Honiton may be chosen.   The Raleigh-bar stitch, point de Bruxelles, and "spiders" may be used in following the outlines given for stitches.

No. 44.

CORNER IN MODERN LACE.

The suggestions given above will also apply to this design, which may be used for a table spread, or a handkerchief, according to the braid selected. As illustrated, the design is of pretty dimensions for a doily or a toilet-cushion cover, or for a handkerchief. All of the bar work seen may be done with single threads instead of the complete Raleigh method, and the rosettes or "spiders" may be larger or smaller as preferred.

No. 44.—Design for Modern Lace.

No. 45.—Corner in Modern Lace.

No. 46.

PILLOW-SHAM OF BATTENBURG LACE AND LINEN.

A very elaborate pillow-sham is here illustrated. It is made of Battenburg braid and appropriate thread, together with an intermingling of rings, and forms one of the most elegant appointments of a handsomely furnished bed-room. The pattern is very distinct and is called the "rose and leaf" design. The ground-work is formed of rings and Raleigh bars, while the centers of the roses and their leaves are filled in in various fancy stitches which include the crosses and rosettes used in drawn-work, Sorrento bars, points de Venise and Bruxelles, d'Alençon bars, etc., etc. If desired the linen square may be made larger, and the lace but one row of blossoms in width. The square is made of the finest household linen and is completed with a broad hem-stitched hem before the lace is added. The lace design may be obtained in any width desired by sending to a professional lace-maker; or, a clever student may be able to enlarge the design herself.

No. 46.—Pillow-Sham of Battenburg Lace and Linen.

No. 47.

DESIGN FOR PRINCESS OR DUCHESSE LACE COLLAR AND CUFFS.

Although this design is represented very small, it is sufficiently clear to convey a good idea of its outlines, and enable a student of average ability to adapt it to collar and cuffs of any size desired. Raleigh bars are used in connecting the various portions of the braids, while any of the fine stitches preferred may be chosen to fill in around the loops of the blossoms and foliage. A fine picot braid finishes the edge.

No. 48.

ENGLISH NEEDLE-POINT LACE.

This engraving illustrates a very beautiful specimen of modern-point lace in a design combining the lily and the rose. Raleigh bars and buttons render the heavy part of the work effective, while the daintier point stitches and bars are used to fill in the floral sections—coarse and fine thread being used in the work.

This lace, like any of the varieties now fashionable may be made wide or narrow, or fine or coarse by designs furnished as required by lace-makers in general; and the patterns may also be developed in silk or ribbon needle-point, which is a style of ornamentation appearing extensively as a decoration for scarfs, piano and table covers, mantel valences, etc., etc.

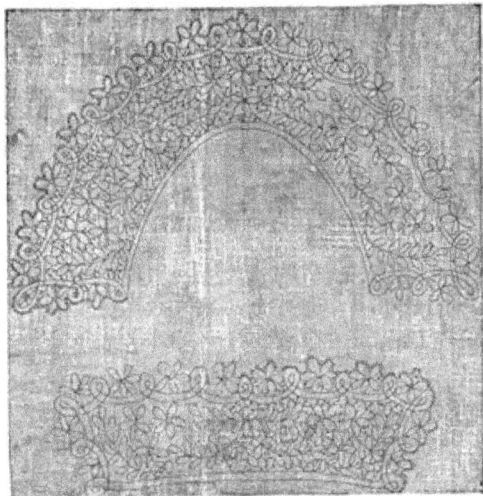

No. 47. DESIGN FOR PRINCESS OR DUCHESSE LACE COLLAR AND CUFFS.

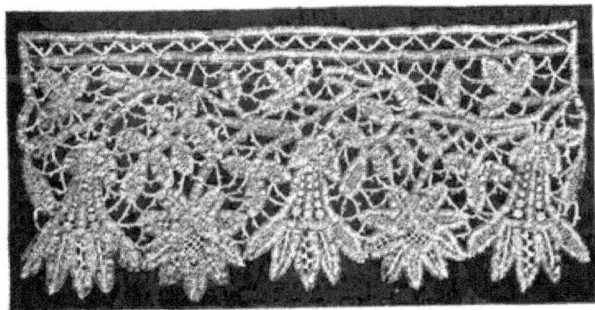

No. 48.—ENGLISH NEEDLE-POINT LACE.

No. 49.

ROYAL BATTENBURG LACE.

This design was among the first ones of this lace to appear, and is fully entitled to its royal name. Fancy Battenburg braid was selected for the foundation, and various stitches chosen for filling-in purposes. Among the stitches are point de Bruxelles, made similarly to the Italian lace stitch, point de fillet, plain Raleigh bars, point d'Alençon, rosettes, rings and point de Grecque. The central figure conveys a hint of the outlines of the royal crown, and the lace is really sumptuous in design and texture. In 1883, Mrs. Grace McCormick, the originator of the design and lace was awarded a diploma for her work which was forwarded from Washington, where she applied for a patent for her specimens of Royal Battenburg lace, of which this is one.

No. 49.—ROYAL BATTENBURG LACE.

No. 50.

ROMAN LACE (CORAL PATTERN).

The design here given is for a lappet or scarf-end, and will afford a suggestion for the making of larger articles or edging in similar arrangements of braid. It will be observed that the braid forms irregular lines that recall the branchings of coral, and it will be a very easy matter for an amateur lace-maker to similarly arrange her braid for any purpose she desires. Fine Raleigh bars form the connecting work, and a button-hole picot-finish is made along the edge of the braid which forms the border. In making an edging, a definite outline could be kept for the lower edge, and above this an irregular or indefinite outline arranged.

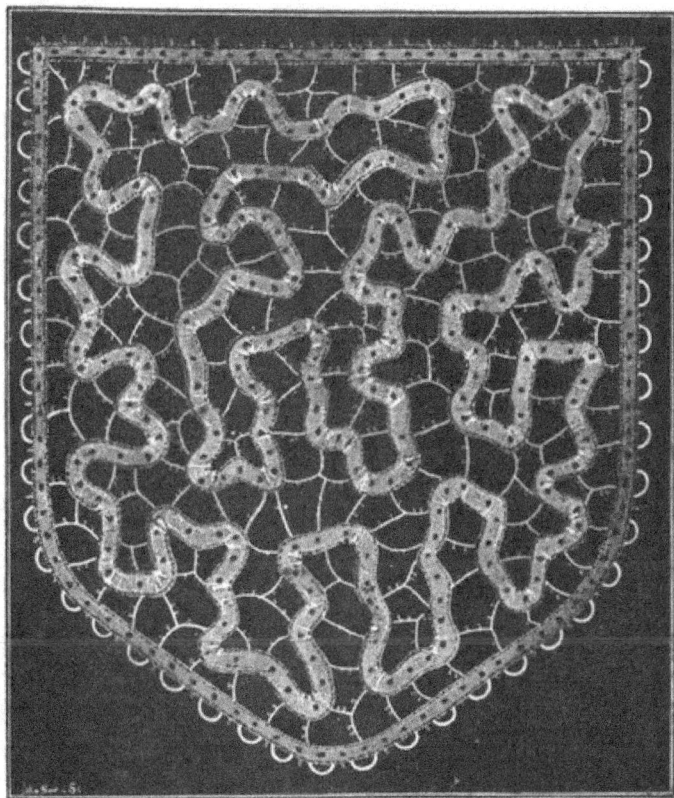

No. 50.—ROMAN LACE (CORAL PATTERN).

No. 51.

TIDY OF BATTENBURG LACE.

The tidy here illustrated is made entirely of Battenburg lace, and is a beautiful specimen of this kind of work. The border design is the same as the one previously described for a pillow-sham, except that but one row of the blossoms and foliage is used. The center is composed of rows of braid crossed to form squares or open spaces that are filled in with rosettes in point d'Angleterre. This center is attached to the braid at the inner edge of the border by a series of bars arranged in d'Alençon style and then wrought with the thread after the method used in d'Anvers bars. This tidy, enlarged, forms an elegant design for a pillow-sham. When laid over a tinted silk spread or pillow, a sham of this design shows its full beauty. When the braid is basted on in the outlines desired, the remainder of the work will be a pleasing pastime, as none of it is so fine as to require very close attention.

No. 51.—Tidy of Battenburg Lace.

No. 52.

MODERN LACE.

A handsome specimen of lace is here illustrated. It will be observed that the braid from which it is made is woven like fine binding braid, and in this respect differs from any of the lace-braids herein illustrated. It will also be seen that no two figures of the design are alike, and that various stitches are used in completing them, many being combinations of or adaptations from the stitches illustrated at the beginning of this pamphlet. The engraving is sufficiently plain to enable the worker to decide which stitches are used alone or in combination, and to guide her correctly in their application. The picot-edge is done in point de Venise stitch.

No. 53.

MODERN-POINT LACE EDGING.

This is an easy design to follow and is simply made. Heavy Sorrento bars with picot loops form the ground-work, while the filling-in stitches are of the same class done in fine thread in regular squares and also a combination of point de fillet and point de Grecque. A dainty picot-finish is added at the lower edge. This edging is pretty for bordering draperies or decorating dresses, and may be made as fine or as coarse as desired.

No. 52.—Modern Lace.

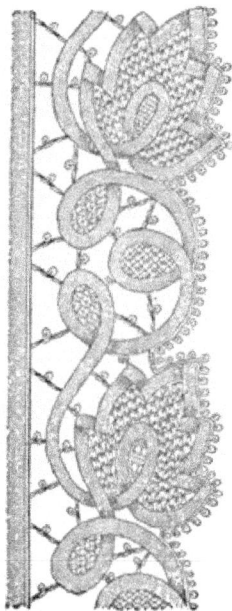

No. 53.—Modern-Point Lace Edging.

No. 54.

SQUARE IN MODERN-POINT LACE.

In this design will be observed a favorite combination—the rose and the butterfly. Close inspection will also disclose that the filling-in stitches are of a diverse character, and that to this diversification much of the beauty of the work is due. As most of the stitches are easily recognized, and as the copyist can easily adapt methods for the combinations seen, it will not be necessary to definitely describe them.

The square may be used for a scarf-end in connection with the edging No. 53 seen on page 91, if the braid selected is sufficiently fine. When coarser braid is chosen, the square will be pretty for doilies, tidies or the center of a table spread. The design may be daintily made up of ribbon, with silk for the stitches. In this event it may be set into a scarf or drapery of China or Surah silk with charming results.

No. 54—Square in Modern-Point Lace.

No. 55.

LOUIS XIV. CURTAIN-LACE.

This is a very popular decoration for curtains and vestibule doors and is made of heavy écru or white net and braid. The design selected is generally a border with a corner piece, and sometimes a center piece. The specimen here given is simply a square of the net decorated as illustrated to convey an idea of this at present fashionable curtain lace. The design is first traced on tracing cloth that is then underlaid with brown paper to hold it stiffly in place. The net is then laid over this and smoothly basted down so that the tracing shows through plainly. Then écru or white Battenburg braid is used to follow the design, and is shaped into the leaves and flowers seen, rings being used for the centers of the blossoms and écru or white cord for the stems. The net is cut from under the rings at the centers of the large roses, and each opening is filled in with point de fillet and English wheels. The effect is very rich and the work is not difficult to do.

When a curtain is thus embroidered or decorated with braid, it is bordered the same as the square illustrated, or upon that principle, with rows and points of Battenburg braid. Ribbon is often used in this way for tidies, bureau scarfs and various other little household decorations, and in this event the flower and foliage tints may be carried out in the design.

No. 55.—LOUIS XIV. CURTAIN-LACE.

DARNED-NET SCARFS, KERCHIEFS, TIDIES, EDGINGS, INSERTIONS, ETC., ETC., WITH DESIGNS FOR THE SAME AND OTHER ARTICLES.

Bobbin net, or "bobbinet," or "net" as it is now commonly called, was first made by machinery in 1809, and was so called because the threads from which it was made were wound upon bobbins, and *twisted* into meshes instead of being *looped* in knitting style as they were previous to the invention of the machine. The latter was invented by John Heathcoat, the son of an English farmer; but to France must be given the credit of introducing the "darned work" by which some of its costliest net laces were first made. From these laces originated the industry of darning net by machinery and by hand, and in all grades from fine silk-blonde and Brussels net to the coarsest wash net, such as is used for curtains and draperies.

In the earlier days the pattern was stamped on the net by means of wooden blocks, and the net was then placed in a frame, and the darner with her left hand under the lace followed the design with her needle and cotton, linen or silk floss held over the work in the right hand. This method may be employed at the present time; or, the design may be drawn on thick paper and the net basted over it; or, if the net is coarse the design may be followed by counting the meshes and inserting the needle and floss accordingly; or the design may be transferred to the net itself by black or colored pencils, or stamping. The darner must decide for herself which method for holding the work she will use. Some of the most expert darners simply hold the net loosely in their hands and copy the design by eye alone. Wash-silk floss, India floss which is of linen but looks like silk, and ordinary darning flosses are all used for this work. Darned net is liked for many purposes, as will be observed by the variety of designs and illustrations given on these pages.

No. 1.

SCARF-END OF DARNED NET.

This illustration pictures a very pretty scarf-end, but presents it only half of its actual width. The scarf is about a yard in length and is darned with linen floss and edged with the finest feather-edge braid. The center portions of the flowers and foliage are cut out after the solid darning is made, and the spaces are then filled in with a fancy mesh done with fine cotton in point de Bruxelles stitch.

No. 1.—Scarf-End of Darned Net (Half Size).

No. 2.

NARROW CUFF OF DARNED NET.

This engraving presents a cuff of darned net in its actual width. The design is also suitable for an edging and may be easily changed into an insertion. Feather-edge braid is used to complete the cuff. A collar may be made to match if desired.

No. 3.

CORNER OF KERCHIEF OF DARNED NET.

This kerchief is made similarly to the scarf-end illustrated on page 97, and as represented, the corner is only one-half its actual size. The kerchief itself is about twenty-two inches square and is very dainty in effect. The stars which fill in the central portion are very simple to make, and the eyelets in each are punched with a bodkin and then worked once around in point de Bruxelles or button-hole stitch. The kerchief is made of fine Brussels net and the darning is done with India floss.

No. 2.—Narrow Cuff of Darned Net.

No. 3.—Corner of Kerchief of Darned Net (Half Size).

No. 4.

TIDY OF DARNED NET.

This engraving represents a charming little tidy made of coarse wash-net darned with wash-silk floss in Oriental colorings. The tidy has an inch wide hem and is about eleven inches wide and twelve long. The hem is fastened down by three rows of darning stitches, the outer row being deep garnet, the middle row bright old-rose and the inner row deep orange. One small fan is made of the orange and pale-blue, another of the old-rose with sulphur-yellow, and the third peacock-blue and crimson. One large fan is made of pale-pink and silver-gray (darned together), and wood-brown; another is made of the garnet and the sulphur-yellow, while the third is made of orange and pale-blue. The scrolls meeting at the center are made, one of wood-brown, one of sulphur-yellow and one of garnet, and the rest of the design is made in different shades of dull green. Laid over white, this tidy is very effective. It may be darned in one color on white, black or écru net if preferred, and with linen floss.

No. 4.—Tidy of Darned Net.

No. 5.

TIE-END OF DARNED NET.

A tie-end in its actual width is here illustrated. The tie is about three-quarters of a yard long, and is darned in all-over style in the design seen in the engraving, with linen floss. A line of fine feather-edge braid finishes the tie in a dainty manner. This design may be used for any other article preferred, and its details will also suggest other designs of a similar character which may be invented by the worker. This scarf as well as the others just described, may be made up in black if preferred; and in this event it will be easier for the darner to follow the meshes if she bastes her net over a white background. The design may or not be traced on this background.

No. 5.—Tie-End of Darned Net (Full Width).

No. 6.

DARNED-NET EDGING, WITH OVER-WROUGHT STITCH.

This handsome edging is darned upon a wide strip of net with coarse and fine embroidery cotton, and after the pattern is completed the lower edge of the net is cut away. The coarse cotton is used to outline the design and fill in some of the central portions, while the fine is darned in between the outer and center portions, and is used for the over-wrought portions. These portions are " run " back and forth loosely to form a raised foundation for the buds and rose-centers before the over-wrought work is done. The edging is given full-size and no difficulty will be experienced in following the design or making the lace ; and the design may be adapted to any article of wear that can be made of darned net. A scarf or kerchief, dotted with rosebuds made like those of this design would be a very dainty article of personal adornment ; and the buds might be made of pale-pink or yellow floss with a charming effect. The floral idea might be further carried out by using shaded green floss for the foliage.

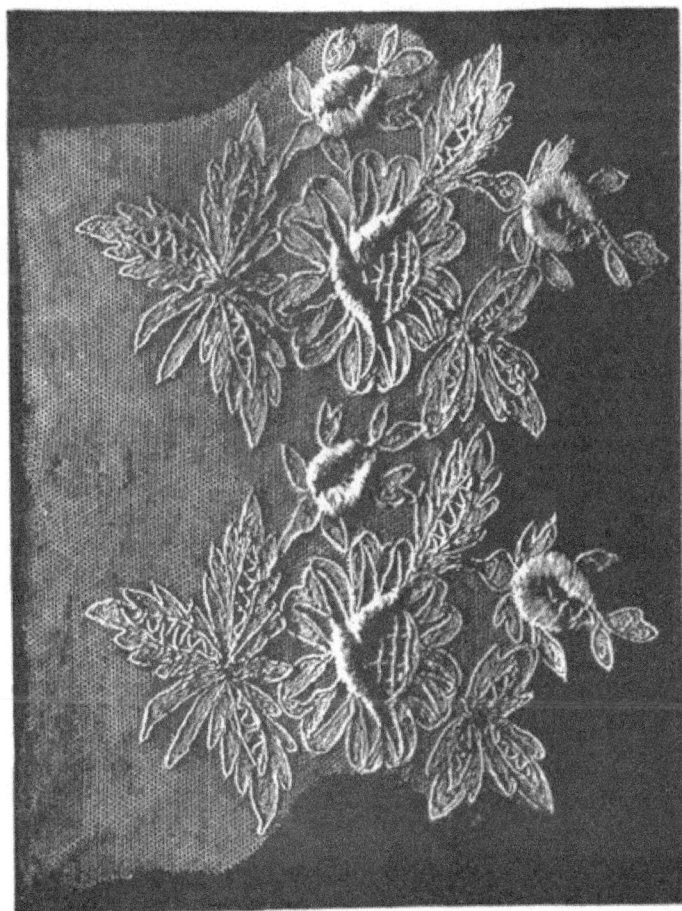

No. 6.—Darned-Net Edging, with Overwrought Stitch (Full Size).

Nos. 7 and 8.

DARNED-NET EDGINGS.

It will not be necessary to give special instructions for either of the edgings here illustrated, as both are given full size and the designs are perfectly distinct. No. 7 is finished with a button-holed scallop from which the net is cut away when the work is completed. Either edging may be made of white, écru or black net as preferred, and the floss may be white or tinted, or of cotton, linen or silk.

In making No. 8 upon black net, silver or gilt thread or colored flosses will be found very effective. Black net thus darned is very pretty for ruching and jabots for dress-waists.

In making darned edgings, net may be purchased in various edging widths, and in this style is often called "footing." When 'bobbin net (or bobbinet as it is now called) was first invented, it was made only one inch wide but now it may be purchased three and one-half yards wide if desired.

No. 7.—Darned-Net Edging.

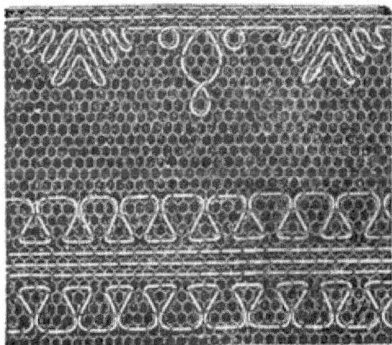

No. 8.—Darned-Net Edging.

No. 9.

PILLOW-SHAM OF DARNED NET.

This engraving represents one of the many uses to which darned net is put. Moderately coarse net was selected, and the darning was done with linen floss in the various patterns seen, and which are repeated in a larger form on the following pages. The sham was hemmed after the darning was finished, and a frill of darned-net edging was then added. Tinted silk or sateen should be laid under such a sham in order to bring out the beauty of the work. The ambitious darner may make a bed-spread to correspond with her shams, if she has the time to devote to the task and the patience to complete it; and in making such a set, she need not confine herself to the designs here given, but may select any others she admires, or may originate a design herself. Individual ideas as to decoration so widely differ, that clever workers are sure to evolve designs of various characters and a generally uniform beauty. Blossoms, leaves, carvings, Oriental figures, brocades, etc., etc., all afford dainty ideas for designs for darned net.

No. 9.—Pillow-Sham of Darned Net.

No. 10.

CENTER OF PILLOW-SHAM.

This engraving presents an enlarged representation of the center of the pillow-sham seen on page 109, and also shows its suitability for the center of a tidy. The inner design is very easy to follow, as will be seen by referring to No. 12 on page 113, where a large illustration of it is seen supplemented by a vine-border at each side. The outer border of this center-piece is very simple, and may be darned in diamonds as large or as small as desired.

No. 11.

SECTION OF PILLOW-SHAM.

In looking at the sham illustrated on page 109, the design illustrated at No. 11 will be seen at either side of the middle-stripe design. As here represented it will be easy to copy either for a pillow-sham or for any article of decoration or personal use desired. The ingenious worker will find many methods of combining it with other designs or applying it as an insertion, a border or an edging ; and she may also use her own taste as to darning with white or colored floss, or using white, écru, fancy-colored or black net.

No. 10.—Center of Pillow-Sham.

No. 11.—Section of Pillow-Sham.

No. 12.

SECTION OF PILLOW-SHAM.

This design has been mentioned in connection with the pillow-sham seen upon page 109, and the engraving represents it perfectly. It may be employed for the purpose mentioned or adapted to any other use required, and may be copied exactly or varied to suit individual taste. Black net darned with gold thread in this design would be pretty for decorating a black silk gown or trimming a black hat.

No. 13.

SECTION OF PILLOW-SHAM.

Another portion of the pillow-sham mentioned is here illustrated, but the design is quite as appropriate for any other decorative purpose. Yokes for night-dresses may be darned in this pattern, or in any of the ones previously given, with a very pretty effect ; and when tinted ribbon, mull or lawn is laid under the darned stripes, the effect is very dainty indeed. Yokes to children's dresses may also be darned in this pattern or the others, and little caps or hoods may be made to match and lined with a tinted or white fabric.

No. 12.—Section of Pillow-Sham.

No. 13.—Section of Pillow-Sham.

No. 14.

END OF DRAPERY-SCARF OF DARNED NET.

The end of the drapery-scarf from which this engraving was made is about fourteen inches square, and the sides are turned under for about a quarter of an inch, or a little more, and darned down closely to represent a selvedge. The design is Oriental in outline and is easy to follow. As represented the scarf is made of white net and darned with white linen floss; but the Oriental effect may be carried out more perfectly if the darning is done with colored flosses with an intermingling of silver or gilt thread. White, black, écru or colored net may be used. Two ends are made and then gathered to a smaller square of net. This small square is then drawn together through the center under a bow of wide satin ribbon, and the scarf is then fastened to the article of furniture it is to decorate. To its ends may be added tassels, rings or any edge-finish that is in accord with the materials of the scarf. Black net darned with gold, crimson, peacock-blue, and pale-yellow and pale-olive, results in a charmingly Eastern or Oriental effect.

No. 14.—END OF DRAPERY-SCARF OF DARNED NET.

No. 15.

DESIGN FOR A CORNER OR SQUARE OF DARNED NET.

A very pretty design, as simple as it is effective, is here represented. According to the purpose for which the work is intended, and the color of the net selected, the darning may be done in cotton, linen or silk, and in white, black, écru or colors. The pattern may be modified in any way pleasing to the taste, or diversified by the introduction of portions of other designs or individual ideas.

No. 16.

BORDER FOR DARNED NET.

A pretty border for tidies, draperies, flounces, yokes, collars or any article requiring a border is here illustrated. Any of the suggestions given above may be adopted in making this border, which may be used separately or in combination with other borders, according to individual taste. Gold thread upon black or white net would, in this design, result in a very effective dress decoration.

No. 15.—DESIGN FOR A CORNER OR SQUARE OF DARNED NET.

No. 16.—BORDER FOR DARNED NET.

No. 17.

DESIGN FOR DARNED NET.

This pretty pattern may be used as a border, insertion or stripe for personal or household articles, and is one of the most popular designs in use. It is very easy to follow and is illustrated full size. It might be used to border the lower edge of a wide flounce for a petticoat, or, with equal propriety, applied to a tidy or a window drapery, providing the worker regulates the size of the design appropriately for the work in hand. For window draperies it would need to be much broader and larger in other ways than as represented.

No. 18.

EDGING OF DARNED NET.

The design here presented is of full size, and very easy to work. A dainty edge in button-hole stitch is worked for the border, and the net is afterward cut out to form the tiny scallops. This is a pretty pattern for neck and wrist frills, jabots or ruffles, or for the adornment of ker-chiefs for the neck or pockets, or for any purpose for which lace edging is selected.

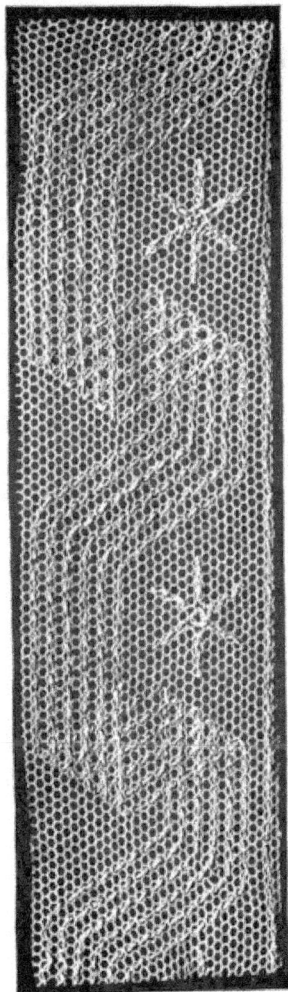

No. 17.—DESIGN FOR DARNED NET.

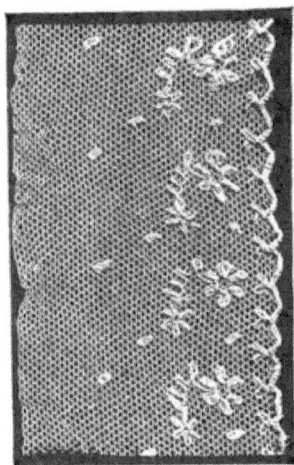

No. 18.—EDGING OF DARNED NET.

No. 19.

DESIGN FOR DARNED NET.

This engraving represents a flounce of darned-net in its actual size or width.   It will be seen that the design is simple, but at the same time very effective.   The flounce is for a child's dress made of net darned all over in the pattern seen in the picture, and worn over a tinted silk slip.   The all-over work is very pretty indeed, and the design may be put to any of the many uses for which darned net is suitable.   It is pretty for yokes, pillow-shams, counterpanes, infants' dresses and carriage-robes, parasol-covers, sofa-pillow covers, and in fact for any article that may be made of lace.

The points of the flounce are darned back and forth in selvedge effect ; but they may be worked in button-hole stitch if preferred.   A touch of color may be given the work by using a little tinted or colored floss with the white, though the latter is most generally selected for darning net.   In using tints, more delicate shades will be found in silk darning-flosses.

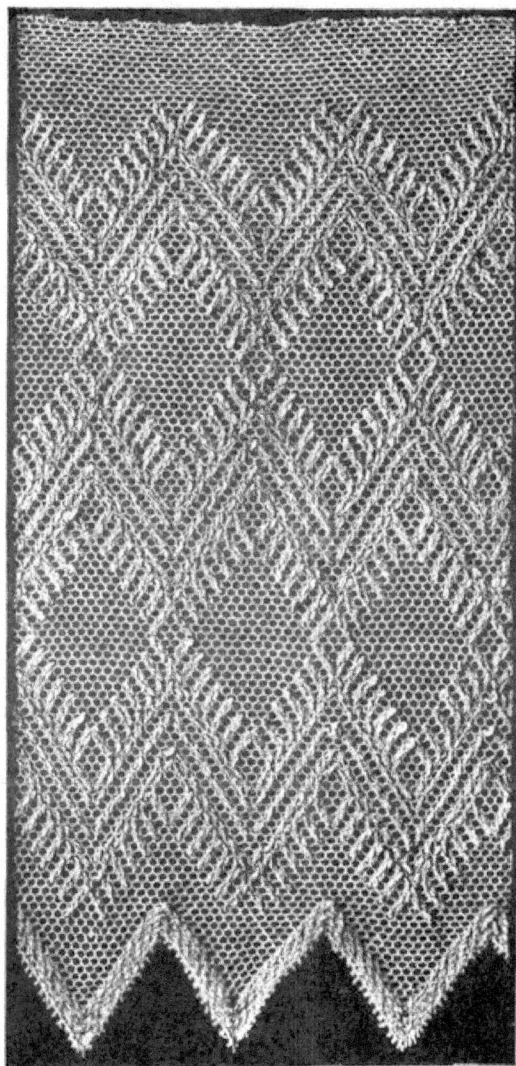

No. 19.—DESIGN FOR DARNED NET.

No. 20.

DESIGN IN DARNED NET.

This design is extremely simple, and it may be used separately as a border or insertion, or in combination with parts of other designs in making up a large or elaborately-worked article. It is dainty enough for the decoration of an infant's garment if desired for such ornamentation, or heavy enough for elaborating an adult's attire.

No. 21.

DESIGN FOR A YOKE OR SECTION OF A GARMENT IN DARNED NET.

The yoke, sleeves, collar, cuffs and flounce of a child's dress were beautifully darned in the design illustrated by this engraving, and the effect was far more charming than can be conveyed by a picture. The little gown was airy enough for a sprite, and its greatest cost was in the outlay of the time devoted to its construction; and even this could not be counted a real outlay, as only odd moments of leisure were employed in making the pretty garment. White net, white floss and white India lawn were the composing materials.

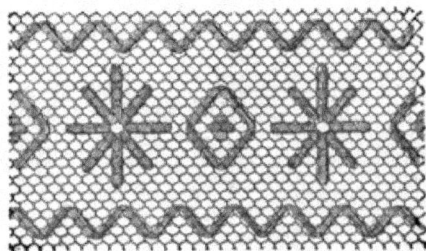

No. 20.—Design in Darned Net.

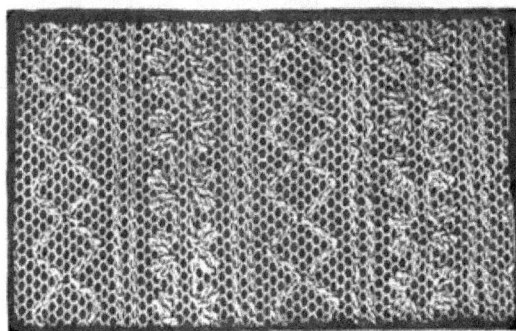

No. 21.—Design for a Yoke or Section of a Garment in Darned Net.

Nos. 22 and 23.

DESIGNS FOR DARNED NET.

Both of these designs are very pretty for diverse purposes, and also very easy to follow. Either may be used as a heading, an insertion or a border, separately or in conjunction with other designs. Many of the suggestions given concerning other designs upon previous pages will apply to these two designs, which fact leaves little to suggest for them individually. Each darner will think out for herself many uses to which to put designs, many combinations in which they will prove effective, and many colorings suggested by the tints which govern her room or her wardrobe; all of which would be an impossible task for any one person, unacquainted with the surroundings of all our students to accomplish. One idea from one person will suggest another idea to a second person, and thus, in the lace-work at the beginning and after part of this book, as in all fancy work, upon an evolution of ideas must rest the great responsibility of an endless variety of designs.

No. 22.—Design for Darned Net.

No. 23.—Design for Darned Net.

www.ingramcontent.com/pod-product-compliance
Lightning Source LLC
Chambersburg PA
CBHW030619270326
41927CB00007B/1239